Memoir
of a
Useless Boy

To Margaret

All the very best for your "retirement".

Many, many thanks for your guidance, leadership and support.

Paul.

Memoir of a Useless Boy

S. Leonard Syme, Ph.D.

Professor of Epidemiology and Community Health (Emeritus)
School of Public Health
University of California, Berkeley

To order additional copies of this book, contact:
Xlibris Corporation
1-888-795-4274
www.Xlibris.com
Orders@Xlibris.com
101467

Contents

Dedicated to my unbelievably talented and
wonderful grandchildren

Christopher, Nolan, Melanie, and Jenna

They make it all worthwhile.

1

THE ROAD LESS TRAVELED BY

It was a bizarre way to behave. I still behave that way now, fifty-six years later. I think I am now beginning to understand some of the reasons. In 1955, I was a graduate student at UCLA working on my master's degree in sociology. Once a week during the fall semester, I attended a remarkable seminar, along with twelve other graduate students, dealing with the topic of urban sociology. Our professor, Eshref Shevsky, was the man who had developed a new way to study cities. His method was called social area analysis. He was a famous and distinguished scholar, and we all felt very privileged to be able to study with him. I recall, as if it was yesterday, my strange behavior in that seminar. All the students in the room were brilliant and very serious. We had all worked hard to prepare for each class session. Every week, Professor Shevsky would call upon each of us to explain a particular concept, describe the research evidence, and reach a conclusion. I recall listening to my fellow students and saying to myself, "I need to do a better job than they are doing. I need to come up with an original idea about this or, at least, a different way to frame the discussion. I need to carve my *own* path."

Years later, I read a poem by Robert Frost and immediately recognized what he meant by saying, "Two roads diverged in a wood, and I—I took the one less traveled by. And that has made all the difference." In the years it has taken to write this memoir, I am beginning see why I felt that way then, and why, as an emeritus professor with no ambitions for personal advancement or need for recognition, I still have those feelings. I have never been a competitive person. I have never been ambitious either. Why then did I behave in this otherwise inexplicable way?

In my memoir, I try to explain why I needed to find my own way in order to survive a dangerous and stifling early life. I also try to document one of the consequences of this struggle: a career that has focused on the importance of social forces in influencing health and well-being. While this idea sounds obvious now, it was not when I began to work in this field in 1957. In those days, the factors that were understood to affect health were having favorable genes, receiving competent medical care, and behaving in healthy ways. My work has attempted to reframe the discussion to suggest the importance also of the social environment. During my research career, the evidence has now accumulated sufficiently to show that a healthy social environment may be even more important than the factors we already knew about. When I began this work, the concept of social determinants was a radical, highly unconventional, and quite controversial idea. In those early days, I was one of the leaders of this new way of thinking, but I had no idea that my rebellious approach was so clearly a product of childhood years in a battlefield.

I describe all this as if I had everything neatly in mind at the beginning. I did not. I began writing this memoir in Paris during the summer of 2004. The first words consisted of twelve pages that described my experiences in dealing with a very challenging early life. A year later, also in Paris, I added details to the story. Several months after that, I expanded the writing to include my adult life. As these pages accumulated, I was beginning to see a second story emerging. It was turning out that my escape from a traumatic early life—to me, an interesting story in its own right—was also providing some insight into why I chose to pursue the research that I did for the rest of my life. I was not conscious of any of this. It is only in retrospect that I am beginning to see a pattern linking the two.

As a result of this recognition, I have written a memoir with two interrelated themes. One theme describes several events that helped me escape from a childhood environment to a life of accomplishment. The second theme describes how that escape was instrumental in helping me to create a new scholarly discipline, social epidemiology, that now has international recognition and significance. I did not come up with this idea myself, of course. Late in the nineteenth century, Louis Villerme, Rudolph Virchow, Edgar Sydenstricker, and, my hero, Emile Durkheim, pointed out that factors in the social environment had an important impact on health. When I first began my work on these issues, the thinking of those early pioneers was just beginning to be taken seriously, but aside from the research of my colleague John Cassel at the University of North Carolina, there was virtually nothing being done to follow up on those ideas.

So now, at the age of seventy-nine, I am finally beginning to understand what many psychologists have long known: the choices and decisions that we make in our lives often are a consequence of a childhood issue that was never resolved. In my case, it was two things: (1) being branded with the label of being a useless child and (2) living in a threatening environment where escape was the only way to survive. I am only now beginning to see how those early life circumstances shaped the rest of my life in ways that hopefully have made a difference.

2

ON BEING A USELESS BOY

I didn't realize it at the time, but that hot day in June 1946 was to set the course for what I did the rest of my life. I was fourteen years old, and I was living in Winnipeg, Manitoba. The Second World War had just ended, and there was a building boom going on to provide housing for returning Canadian veterans. As part of that explosion of building, my dad, an electrical contractor, was installing the electrical service for 110 houses in the North End of the city. He came into my bedroom one morning and said, "I need your help on a job. It will take a couple of weeks to do it. If you do good work, I'll pay you. Put on your clothes and let's go." He needed my help because he only had two men working for him that day. He was always short of helpers because he fired them so soon after he hired them. The workers he employed never worked hard enough or fast enough or good enough and he always ended up doing all the work himself. This job was one of the biggest he ever had, though, and he really did need help if he was going to keep on schedule. I was a skinny young kid, and I was not very good at manual labor, but he was running out of options. My job was to install hundreds of plugs and switches in these buildings. All the wires had already been put into the houses; all I had to do was connect the wires to the plugs and switches, fit them into the boxes that already had been placed in the walls, and then screw the covers to the wall.

When we arrived at the job, I was given an old tool belt, and I loaded it with the tools I would need that day. "There are," he said, "only two rules." One rule was that the wires had to be wound around the screws in a clockwise fashion. This was to ensure that when the screw was tightened in a clockwise direction, the screw would tighten the connection, not loosen it. "The second rule," he said, was that I had to "run from plug to plug and from switch to switch and from house to house. No walking."

I set about my task with a determination to do my job well. I almost never was able to do a job well enough to please my dad, but I thought I had a real chance this time. I knew what I was supposed to do, and I thought I might at last prove myself worthy in his eyes. Perhaps the other workers he hired had failed, but this time I thought I really had a chance. The day got hotter and hotter, but I worked all day long at a frantic pace, and at the end of the long day, I sank to the floor in the living room of one of the houses, exhausted but with a happy smile on my face.

I heard my father walking into the house where I was sitting. I had been nervously awaiting his arrival. He said he was now going to inspect the work I had done that day. He left the room I was in. I could hear him moving from the bedroom to the bathroom and then to the dining room. Finally, he came back into the living room where I was recuperating. He said, "You are a useless person who can't be counted on to do any good work." It turned out that there was a third rule that he hadn't told me about. The third rule was so obvious that he didn't think it needed mentioning. The third rule was that the slots on the screws that fastened the plates to the wall had to be aligned, either horizontally or vertically to the floor. The slots on my screws were pointing in all directions. "You obviously don't care about your work," he said. "What kind of worker leaves his work as sloppy as you did?" he asked. A useless worker, I said to myself, that's who. I was then instructed to pack up, get in his truck, and leave for home.

I don't mean to focus too much attention on improperly installed screws. I was useless in many other ways. In addition to my sloppy work with the screws, I also was useless in dealing properly with the caps on bottles of soda. One of my father's favorite games was to challenge me to a bottle-top crushing competition. He would take the metal top of a soda bottle and crush it between his thumb and forefinger. Then he would say, "Now you do that!" As a young boy, there was no way I could do that. Of course, I have secretly tried—many times—to do that little trick even as a mature adult, and I have never succeeded. He really had strong fingers.

My father and me

Yet another failure was the width of my shoulders. I can't tell you how many times I heard my father complain to anyone who would listen about the fact that I had narrow shoulders. "A real man has broad shoulders. When I was your age, my shoulders were as broad as they are now!" He made it very clear that I was deficient in the shoulder department. Not only was I a failure regarding shoulders, but I was deficient as a real man. As I grew older, my shoulders broadened out, but by then the message had sunk in.

At my advanced age, it is a little unsettling to recognize that virtually every decision I have made in my life was to show that I am not useless. While I didn't realize it, I now see that I have devoted my life to proving my father wrong. Of course, I have put a more positive spin on this. I say to myself, and others, that I want to make a difference in the world. But lurking behind this noble sentiment is a more basic and less elegant need: a compelling need to be seen as not useless.

During my working life, I had only occasionally given thought to these ideas. But one Sunday morning, my daughter Karen called to say, "I have something I want to say to you, Dad. And I want you to hear me out, listen to everything I have to say before you argue with me." I tensed for the worst. She then said, "I have just read two autobiographies that completely absorbed me." Where was this going? I knew she read a lot. She then dropped the other shoe. "Both of these books made me think of your childhood, Dad, and I couldn't help but think of the compelling and inspiring tale that you could tell of your experiences." She then reminded me that all through her life, she had been on the receiving end of truly countless numbers of people who had told her how her father had changed their lives. She said that I had to write about my childhood and how I came to be the teacher and mentor that I had become. She encouraged me by saying that we could work on this book together.

I hesitated for several weeks before responding to her. I told her that I was reluctant to proceed with the memoir idea because many people have had to overcome difficulties in their early years. That, I said, was not a very interesting theme to write about. She responded by saying that there was more to my story than merely overcoming early difficulties. She reminded me that we had recently had a conversation in which I told her that beyond overcoming early difficulties in my life, and beyond avoiding the "useless" label, I had expressed a strong commitment to make a difference in the world.

I finally agreed to do this writing for two reasons. One reason is that, as a public health researcher, I have for years been interested in understanding how children from disadvantaged backgrounds were able to survive to lead healthy and fulfilling lives. In my research field, this is one of the most compelling issues we must think about. What allows some to escape and thrive? I thought that my story might be useful in shedding some light on this important question. The second reason is more personal. I am curious to know how a useless kid became useful, and I hope that my story may be of interest to my grandchildren as they attempt to understand their family origins.

Shortly after this conversation, I left California to spend another July in Paris. It was during that month away from home that I began to think about whether or not I had really made a difference. As part of my ruminations, I remembered the day I got a phone call from my friend, Bruce Link. Bruce is a professor at the School of Public Health at Columbia University. Bruce said that he and some friends had been discussing how to mentor their graduate students, and they decided to invite the best mentor they knew to come to Columbia to give a talk on the subject. He then said, "We unanimously decided you were the person we wanted to hear from." Their research had revealed, he said, "that many of your students are now worldwide leaders in the field." They wondered if I would be willing to share my thoughts on the best strategies to be a good mentor. I was stunned. I have, for over the last forty years, been a professor of epidemiology and community health in the School of Public Health at the University of California at Berkeley, but I had never really thought about my "method" of mentoring. I just did what seemed to be reasonable. Having to sit down and create a lecture about this topic seemed an overwhelming, perhaps impossible, task. But Bruce is a good guy, and so I decided to give it a shot. It turned out to be one of the toughest jobs I have ever done. I actually worked on this lecture for two months! Finally, I began to formulate some ideas, and in the end, I was able to come up with some thoughts and ideas about mentoring. Everyone in the audience at Columbia seemed pleased with my talk, and I, of course, was flattered to have been thought about in this way.

So what did I talk about? I came to realize that mentoring was more than inviting a young person to sit with me and learn what I know. Instead, it involves recognizing and choosing talented young people who may have no idea about their abilities and then challenging them to be the best they can be. It involves helping them realize their talent and assisting them in seeing how they can utilize their skills. It means working with them to see that they are special people. And this approach really works. Many, many of my former students are now doing more amazing and creative things than I ever could have done. That's another secret of good mentoring. Your students should not only be as good as you are. They should be better. I am, in fact, in awe of most of my former students.

I rarely think of myself as being important enough to be invited to fly across the nation to talk about my approach to such things as mentoring. But I remembered flying back from New York after the Columbia talk in a reflective mood, and as we were flying across the country, I recalled another special time in my life many years earlier. In 1995, a group of faculty colleagues at Berkeley marched into my office and announced that they had organized an event to celebrate my retirement. I smile when I say the word "retirement" because I have retired only in the sense that the university no longer pays me a salary. I still teach, advise, and do research. I still come to the office every day. I fly all over the world giving speeches. And I am probably working harder in retirement than I ever did before. My colleagues decided to mark the occasion anyway. What little event did they have in mind? Coffee and cake in the departmental library? Not quite. My friend, Warren Winkelstein, said on behalf of the visiting delegation, "We decided to organize an all-day-and-evening celebration of your retirement." On the appointed day, Friday, September 22, 1995, in front of a very large audience, dozens and dozens of my former students—most coming from distant places from all over the world—gave talks in appreciation of my work.

I recently found the program for that day and was impressed once again at the work and energy that so many people devoted to organizing this event. The title was "Recent Developments in Social Epidemiology: A Symposium in Honor of Professor Emeritus S. Leonard Syme." Inside the program, the names of ten people are listed as members of the "Tribute Committee." The beginning session involved a welcoming speech by the Dean of the School of Public Health (Dr. Patricia Buffler). Following that, eight former students gave talks on the work they were doing and, at 3:15 p.m., there was a panel discussion including all the speakers and me. The back of the program shows a State of California "Resolution" commending me for my "illustrious record of accomplishments" and for "the inspiration and guidance that he has provided to his students." I came across this Retirement Program quite by accident when I was cleaning out the closet in my study at home.

Hundreds of people later attended a dinner party at the University Faculty Club to continue telling stories about how I had affected the course of their professional lives. On the airplane ride back from New York after my mentoring talk, I realized that I had put this retirement event out of my consciousness. I had never really thought about, or consciously realized, that my work had impacted so many people.

While we were over Salt Lake City on that airplane going home, and while I was still reminiscing about these nice things, my seatmate must have wondered why I groaned aloud. I suddenly remembered a specific moment on that Retirement Day. Following the dinner at the Faculty Club, a group of people put on a little show making fun of me. One young woman, Lisa Ota, told of coming home at the end of the day to have dinner with her husband. She asked him how his day went. As he was telling his story, he stopped and said, "Why are you moving your hands in a circle like that? It's as if you want me to speed up my account." She apologized to him by explaining, "Sorry. I just had a meeting with Len." Everyone in the audience laughed at her dead-on imitation of my behavior. The people in the audience obviously knew exactly what she was talking about!

On that airplane returning from New York, I recalled another talk I was invited to give some years earlier. I can't even remember now which university it was! In any event, someone asked me to give a talk on how my career started. When I began to do research in the field of social epidemiology in 1958, there was no "field." Since that beginning, the field of social epidemiology is now an established one in universities both in this country and abroad. People sometimes introduce me as the "Father of Social Epidemiology." It's easy to be the father of a field; all you have to do is show up first. You don't have to be good. Just first. So I gave a little lecture on all this and, I thought, that was the end of it. A month later, one of my postdoctoral fellows, now a faculty member in the School, Dr. Constance Wang, came to my office to announce that, without my knowledge, she had submitted my little history talk to the journal "Epidemiologic Perspectives and Innovations." She thought, she said, "Others would be interested in it." The paper was titled "The Social Determinants of Disease: Some Roots of the Movement." Then, again without my knowledge, the journal took the liberty of inviting two other papers to accompany mine. One paper was by my former student, Sir Michael Marmot. His paper was titled "The Social Determinants of Disease—Some Blossoms." The second paper was by another former student, Dr. Irene Yen. Her paper contained the testimony of dozens of other people who commented on my work. All this fuss was, of course, quite an unexpected, but appreciated, honor.

Adding to this accumulation, I have received several other nice recognitions that I list here for the amusement of my grandchildren. In 1986, I was informed that I had been elected to the Institute of Medicine of the National Academy of Science. This was a big deal. Membership in the IOM is a rare and quite prestigious acknowledgment of one's work. That year also, the Institute for Work and Health in Toronto, Canada established a training fellowship in my name. That was very nice too. Shortly after I retired, I was awarded the Berkeley Citation. This is an award given by Berkeley to people who, they say, have given "distinguished service to the university." I was also awarded the Panunzio Prize as an "Outstanding Emeritus Professor" in the statewide university system. I was honored by the American College of Physicians for "Distinguished Service in Preventive Medicine." And just this year, I was informed that the American Public Health Association had conferred upon me the Wade Hampton Frost Lectureship Award, one of the most prized recognitions in my field. And so on. I'm not going to go on with this list. You get the idea.

For a man who has usually avoided self-analysis and who has been largely oblivious to the idea of "contributions" and self-congratulations, these events have forced me to think about my life in ways I had never done before. It was never my ambition to be famous. I just wanted to do good work, to avoid being seen as useless, and, in the process of doing those things, to make a difference in the world. These "recognition events" were an in-my-face, hard-to-miss, celebration of my work. One can hide, avoid listening, and refuse to read, but in the end, the message begins to sink in. And I now have some thoughts as to why I find all this confronting. Growing up in a working class neighborhood of Winnipeg, one of the most important lessons is to not forget where you came from. Don't act like a big shot. Don't behave as if you are somebody important. Don't put on airs. Be like a normal person. I clearly got the messages I was taught.

3

ONCE UPON A TIME IN DAUPHIN

The capital city of Manitoba is Winnipeg. Back in the time when I was a boy, the city had a population of 250,000. Two hundred miles northwest of Winnipeg was the small town of Dauphin. It had a population of 2,500 people in the 1930s. Main Street was a dirt road. The largest group of people living in Dauphin and its surrounding area came from the Ukraine in the early 1900s. Even today, Ukrainians constitute over 40 percent of Dauphin's population, and almost 30 percent of the residents there still speak Ukrainian. Dauphin began as a wheat-growing center and it still is today. In 1908, my mother was born in this town. She was the only daughter of the most prominent and wealthy family in town. Her father, Eli Bay, had emigrated from a village in the Ukraine some years earlier. As a Jew, he had done this to escape the pogroms initiated by the Ukrainians in his homeland. (A pogrom, for those unfamiliar with the term, refers to the organized mass murder and harassment of Jews in Russia, the Ukraine, and other Eastern European countries during the years 1881-1906.) In a grossly unfair twist of fate, Eli was sent to Dauphin by the Canadian government and he found himself surrounded by the very people from whom he was trying to escape. But Canada was desperate to populate the western part of the country and immigrants had no choice as to where they might land. At about the same time, my grandmother, Gertrude Cherniak, was also sent to this area of Canada. The two met and married shortly thereafter.

Gertrude and Eli Bay

After moving to Dauphin, Eli established an unusual men's clothing store. It is difficult to imagine how he stayed in business. In the middle of a large population of hardworking farmers toiling in a vast wheat growing region, Eli Bay sold the era's fanciest brands of men's clothing: Arrow dress shirts; Pendleton sport shirts; Hart, Shaffner, and Marx suits; Florsheim shoes; Stetson hats. Somehow, his business flourished. (While others now own the store, it is still in business today, almost one hundred years later!) Even though Eli grew up in the Ukraine, the Jews there lived an entirely separate life from the rest of the population and they spoke only Yiddish. In Dauphin, though, Eli learned to speak both

English and Ukrainian, and he developed a loyal customer base that remains to this day. From the humblest of beginnings, Eli became a wealthy man. He and Gertrude built a large house that was the nicest in town. That house later became a funeral home and then a home for nurses in training. It was a big house in a very small town.

Inside Eli and Gertrude's house in Dauphin

Eli and Gertrude had six children: five boys and my mother, Rose. One of the boys, Max, became a pharmacist and came to own his own drugstore in Minneapolis. Another boy, Chuck, attended Harvard and became a very successful businessman in New York City and Los Angeles. Sam became a salesman but died in an automobile accident at the age of twenty-eight. Two other boys, Saul and Harry, worked in the store with the expectation that they would take over when Eli retired.

There were two other Jewish families in town. Max Goffman had a dry goods store next to Eli Bay Ltd. but it sold a more appropriate type of clothing: overalls, straw hats, work gloves, steel-capped shoes. He and his wife, Ann, had two children, both of whom went on to fame and fortune. Their daughter, Frances, became a well-known movie and television star (Frances Bay) who recently was elected into Canada's Walk of Fame. Their son, Erving Goffman, became one of the most famous and influential sociologists in the world. The third Jewish family in town was that of Jake and Bessie Buckwold. Jake also established a business more suited for this farming town: a John Deere tractor store. The Buckwolds had seven children: three boys and four girls.

My mother, Rose, was the only daughter in the family. She had a difficult life in this small community. She had a high school education, but she was completely uninterested in abstract thought and argument. She read magazines and newspapers but mainly for their gossip content. She loved to read about the Royal Family in England. She was not permitted to associate with children who were not Jewish. This prohibition applied especially to Ukrainian non-Jews. As a result, she had a very lonely childhood. As she grew older, this prohibition obviously extended to dating non-Jewish boys. Since so many young men in Dauphin were now out of contention, she was limited to associating with the only four Jewish boys in town. Two of those boys, Percy and Alf Buckwold, were in fact interested in dating her, and even in marrying her, but she found them totally boring. She considered them uninteresting, small-town boys.

My mother

Rose was a very pretty young woman. My grandfather doted on her. But she was bored with life in Dauphin. Her father did everything he could to change that. He gave her a job in the office of his clothing store and he taught her to keep the books. That didn't work. He made sure she had beautiful clothes. That didn't help either. Then, when she was twenty years old, he bought her the most amazing gift ever: a Model A Ford convertible! She may have been the only young lady in Western Canada with such a treasure. That didn't help either.

Rose (in white), her Model A Ford convertible, and friends

Then, one day, a dashing young man descended into the town from Winnipeg and swept her off her feet. My father had arrived! Someone in Winnipeg had told him about this pretty woman from a wealthy family, and they had urged him to contact her. Bob wrote her a letter and took the long, slow, dusty train ride to Dauphin to meet her. She was overwhelmed. He was tall, dark, and handsome and had a movie-star mustache. Many said he looked like John Barrymore. He told jokes, danced well, and knew all the latest songs. He wore multicolored shoes of the latest style, and he was dressed in very fashionable sport jackets. He was charming and very experienced in wooing the ladies. My mother didn't have a chance. They met on February 7, 1931, and were engaged seven days later, on Valentine's Day. On that day, Bob didn't have to take the slow train back to Winnipeg. My mother gave him her car so that he could make the trip to Winnipeg in style and return frequently. No one in Bob's family had ever had a car, so in his mind, he had he had hit the jackpot. He was certainly engaged to the right woman. What a bonanza!

My father

Bob came from a very poor family in Winnipeg. His family had a small house in a very modest district of the city. Max, his father, like Eli Bay, had emigrated from the Ukraine but, unlike Eli, he came with no education and no skills. When the Canadian immigration officer asked Max his name, Max said "Sinelnikov." The immigration official, so the story goes, asked him to spell that difficult name but Max did not know English and he was not an accomplished speller. The immigration officer, a former native of Scotland, gave Max a good Scottish name that, he thought, came fairly close to the words Max had mumbled. Max became Max Syme. Max soon found a job with the Manitoba Telephone Company as a blacksmith. His job was to put shoes on the horses that were used to pull the telephone company wagons. He did not make a lot of money with this job, but it was enough to marry, buy a small house, and begin a family.

Max married Anna and they had five children. One of their sons, Michael, became a distinguished lawyer in Philadelphia and drafted important labor laws that later influenced the law of the land. Michael had a large ranch outside of Philadelphia, with horses. He had emerged from Winnipeg as a major success. Another son, Monte, became a very well-known rabbi in Detroit with a large congregation and a national reputation. Another success. Two daughters, Estelle and Rose, being girls, were not expected to do anything special. They both married unremarkable men and, unfortunately, lived unhappy lives. Estelle married a merchant seaman who was never home. Rose married a very mild-mannered tailor who had a little dry cleaning shop in downtown Winnipeg and who hired me during the summer when I was twelve years old. He died at a young age.

Bob was the problem son. He did not do well in school and he quit after completing grade 8. He never learned to write using cursive letters and was able only to write by printing his words. He was unfamiliar with a life of ideas, and he had no respect for any type of intellectual discourse. He ran away from home at a very young age and he survived for several years by wheeling and dealing and living by his wits. One adventure he had at that time, 1921, involved showing up at the Ford Motor Company in Dearborn, Michigan. He lied about his age—he was fourteen years old at the time—and got a job at the newly completed River Rouge assembly line (the largest integrated factory in the world at that time). That job lasted for one year. Another job he got was to smuggle liquor for Samuel Bronfman who had just established Distillers Corporation Ltd. Bronfman's company would later become Seagram, the largest distiller of alcoholic beverages in the world. My father was involved as a truck driver bringing Bronfman's illegal whiskey from Ontario to New York State during prohibition times. Finally, he got homesick and returned to Winnipeg where his father was able to get him a job as an electrician with the telephone company. It was at this time that Bob's friend told him about the pretty and wealthy girl living in Dauphin. Bob was quick to make the trip there to meet her. He arrived as a shining and eager young man anxious to meet this pretty, lonely young woman.

When they met, Bob was impressed with her beauty and her wealth. And she had this great car. This was a dream come true for him. It was a dream come true for Rose as well. Here was a handsome young man who was willing to get her away from Dauphin and take her to the big city. And he certainly had the gift of gab, as they used to say in those days.

Rose's parents were not as enthusiastic. They thought this uneducated manual worker was simply after their daughter's money. They were not very impressed with his family background either. They warned Rose of all this and told her they would not provide the young couple with financial assistance if she persisted with this marriage obsession. But Rose, the princess, knew these were empty threats and she proceeded to marry the rakish man from the big city who was going to take her away to a life of excitement and glamour. They were married in Dauphin seven months later, on September 6, 1931. In spite of her parents' reservations about the marriage, it was reported by family members that Eli and Gertrude provided Rose with a fabulous and expensive dress and that they put on a lavish wedding ceremony for her. Their hearts were not in it but, everyone said, they had to do this, because how would it look if they didn't? Appearances were everything. After the wedding, Bob and Rose moved to Winnipeg to begin their exciting new life.

My mother Rose, the bride

4

MY MOTHER AND FATHER IN WINNIPEG

The name Winnipeg comes from the Indian Cree word meaning "muddy water." Winnipeg is not an exciting or glamorous city. Almost no one in the United States has ever heard of the place or has any idea where it is located geographically. Winnipeggers take great pride in the fact that the city is at the longitudinal center point of North America! For those who need more information, Winnipeg is north of Minneapolis. It is at the eastern edge of the Canadian prairies. The city has other distinctions. It is the coldest city in North America. Winters are four to five months long with temperatures consistently below freezing during that time. Snow persists all winter, every day. Winds come from the Arctic and result in wind chill temperatures of minus fifty degrees Fahrenheit. On average, fifty-seven days in the winter have temperatures below zero degrees Fahrenheit. Summers are also extreme with many punishing days of very high temperatures and very high humidity. Unfortunately, spring and fall are short, lasting about six weeks each. Winnipeg has another special distinction: larger and more aggressive mosquitoes than anyone has experienced anywhere in the world.

I grew up as a good Jewish boy in a city dominated by Scottish immigrants who brought with them a very strict Presbyterian code of morality. Winnipeg grew as an important population center when, in 1812, Thomas Douglas, the fifth Earl of Selkirk, took pity on the Highland farmers in Scotland who were being forced off their lands ("crofts") to make way for sheep farming. Scottish wool even then was becoming an important export. Lord Selkirk petitioned the British government to settle these farmers in the Red River Valley of Manitoba, but he was turned down. The British government had already given the Hudson's Bay Company that land as part of their fur-trading monopoly. Not to be discouraged by this little problem, Lord Selkirk bought enough shares of the Hudson's Bay Company to assume control of it. He then proceeded to help the displaced highlanders move to Manitoba. This did not go over well with the local Metis native population, but, as we have seen in many other places in the world, the European juggernaut prevailed. A street named in his honor in the North End, my neighborhood, memorializes Lord Selkirk today.

Lord Selkirk's generosity led to the development of a community with a strong Scottish presence and a vibrant Presbyterian sensibility. No shops were permitted to be open on Sunday, there were no Sunday newspapers, and of course, no women were ever permitted to sit in beer parlors! I recall my first visit to racy Minneapolis as a teenager where I was shocked to see that all of these prohibitions were being ignored. During several summers, a group of my friends and I used to go down to Minneapolis to see the traveling group of the New York Metropolitan Opera as they toured "the provinces." I enjoyed the operas but I was astonished by the wild and reckless behavior of the people of Minneapolis. I previously had seen such unseemly behavior in movies but it is quite another thing to see such goings·on in real life. Women sitting in beer parlors (they called them cocktail lounges but I knew better) reading the Sunday papers. We clearly weren't in Winnipeg any longer. The other manifestation of the Scottish presence in Winnipeg was that two of the major sporting venues in the North End were the Scottish lawn bowling club and the curling rink. Holiday events always included traditional highland dancing and pipe band.

Beyond the issues of harsh climate and strict social codes, Winnipeg was a very challenging environment in other ways. Winnipeg is located at the confluence of the Red and Assiniboine rivers. The consequence of this unfortunate location is that the city used to be flooded every spring. On May 8, 1950, a few months before my family left the city forever, a major flood occurred with water above flood stage for fifty·one consecutive days. It was the largest flood ever recorded in Canada. Eight dikes collapsed, four bridges were destroyed, and 100,000 people were evacuated. Following that colossal flood, a whole series of floodways and new dikes were finally built in the city that dramatically reduced the flood danger forever after. My friends and I made quite a bit of money during flood season by looking after pumps that we installed in the basement of homes. We had to work in twenty·four·hour shifts but it was good to help people in those horrendous and scary times. Another way to avoid being seen as useless.

Winnipeg now has a population of over 600,000 people, but during my time, it was much smaller (250,000, as I mentioned earlier). About 40 percent of the population consisted of the descendants of English and Scottish settlers. But more importantly, 15 percent were Ukrainian (all, it seemed, living in my neighborhood). Other groups were French (14 percent), Indian (8 percent) and Jews 2 percent (almost all coming from the Ukraine). The main industry of the city was the transportation of wheat by rail to cities where it could be shipped all over the world.

Rose and Bob came to live in Winnipeg after their wedding. With no financial help from Rose's family, they were forced to rent a tiny apartment on the second floor of a private residence in the North End of the city. Bob's family didn't help either. They didn't help for two reasons. First, they were very poor and had no money to spare. Second, they opposed the marriage because Bob was marrying a fancy girl far above his station instead of sticking to his own kind as everyone expected. Bob's father could not understand his son. "Why didn't you meet a girl from around here and settle down like a normal person?" he asked. The disgraced newlyweds hunkered down in isolation to begin their life together. None of this boded well for them, or for me.

I was born ten months after my parents were married. My mother went back to Dauphin for my birth because she had no friends or relatives in Winnipeg on whom she could count for help. I was born in Dauphin on July 4, 1932. In the Jewish tradition babies are to be named after deceased relatives. This custom is not as strictly adhered to today, but when I was born it was seriously followed. That means taking the whole name. Not one name from one relative and another name from another relative. And no "naming books" so that parents can debate and argue about cute name alternatives. I was named after an uncle who had died a year earlier. His Jewish name was Schmuel Leib. This was translated in English to Sherman Leonard. No one liked the name Sherman, but there was no choice. From the day I was born, therefore, no one ever used the name Sherman for me. I have never liked it either. But my birth certificate shows my first name as Sherman and, therefore, so does my passport. And so do all of my other official documents. I solved this issue by using "S" as my first initial. I don't like people who use first initials. It looks pretentious. But there I am.

Me

My birth somewhat softened the opposition of my mother's parents to this ill-advised marriage and they did provide her with short-term support, shelter and food while she was in Dauphin. But eventually, my mother had to return to Winnipeg and deal with a very difficult situation. She was overwhelmed with the new responsibility of looking after a baby, she was alone because my father was often away for one reason or another, she had no friends to turn to, and she was depressed. She was not able to produce enough milk to breast-feed me. As an infant, I responded to all of this by crying and fussing virtually nonstop. This was not what she had in mind when she ran off to Winnipeg with the dashing stranger to begin her exciting new life.

My mother and me

I am not aware of how my mother dealt with me during my early years, and I must rely on the bits and pieces I picked up from her when she was elderly and reminiscing about the olden days. It was not a pretty story. Basically, she was worn out most of the time, had no support from John Barrymore, and was not able to get advice from girlfriends, or her mother, or from her mother-in-law. And she was not used to the poverty to which she was reduced. She had never experienced this kind of existence ever before. What to do with a constantly fussing, unhappy baby? She did confess to me that she didn't like me. She didn't sing songs to me or read me stories or take me for walks or any of the other things most mothers usually do. When I became a father, I realized that I knew none of the songs and stories that most children know. Because of her troubles with me, she vowed never to have any other babies. As often happens in life, however, my sister, Audrey, was born seven years later.

My mother made many, many trips back to Dauphin in the hopes of finding support there. Perhaps even financial help. By most accounts, I was an adorable baby (when I wasn't crying) and both Rose's mother and father did soften their severe approach a little. Then the situation dramatically changed. The proverbial roof caved in. In 1935, when I was three years old, Eli died of a sudden, massive heart attack. His will specified that Saul and Harry were to take over the store. Max already owned his drugstore in Minneapolis and was doing well. Chuck was given a share of the store, but he wanted to get as far away from Dauphin as he could and he sold his share of the business to his brothers and used that money to finance his MBA studies at the Harvard University School of Business. Eli left the house to Gertrude but specified that the boys were to look after her living expenses forever. Surprisingly, he left a $3,500 insurance policy to his rebellious daughter and her ne'er-do-well husband.

Bob, ever resourceful, thought that with Rose's inheritance and with an invitation to Gertrude to come to live in Winnipeg with them, additional money would finally be forthcoming from the Bay family to help him buy a real house. He knew, of course, that without a house, it would be impossible for Gertrude to come live with them, given their tiny apartment. Gertrude did agree to come as long as Rose and Bob promised that she could have a room of her own. But no one in Dauphin offered any money to help him buy a house.

Bob took this rejection as a challenge. He would show those Bays that he was a better man than they thought he was. A lesser man might have crawled under the bed, but Bob went into action. No bank would loan him money. He knew that. But he did persuade Max Goffman to fund the purchase of a home. Max wanted to honor the memory of his Dauphin friend, Eli. Max had sold his dry goods store in Dauphin and was now a millionaire living in a truly remarkable house in Winnipeg with beautiful, sweeping willow trees on the banks of the Red River. He made his fortune by investing in Winnipeg real estate using funds he got from the sale of his Dauphin dry goods store. Max could barely speak English; he was a crude, obese, cigar-smoking guy, but he was brilliant. He made a fortune (which, fifty years later, is still providing some income for his ninety-year-old actress daughter living in luxury in Los Angeles). Max loaned Bob money for a house and, together with the $3,500 inheritance from Eli, Bob bought a broken-down house at 274 Cathedral Avenue, one block from the little second floor place where he and Rose had been living. The new house had a room for his mother-in-law and his crying son. He then set about repairing and upgrading this house. Somehow, he thought, if he worked hard enough, perhaps he could prove his worth and show them all that he was not simply a money-grubbing playboy.

274 Cathedral Avenue in Winnipeg

So the Goffman loan, the $3,500 inheritance from Eli, and the new house allowed Rose and Bob to invite Gertrude to live with them in Winnipeg. Bob was still working as an electrician at the telephone company but he was also studying day and night to pass the electrical contractor's exam. He finally accomplished that considerable feat and began to remodel and rebuild the house in the evenings and on weekends. It was a two-story house with a full basement. The downstairs consisted of a living room, dining room, and a kitchen. The living room had nice furniture that was always covered in plastic. In fact, the entrance to the living room had a rope across it to limit access. That room was reserved for "company." There were three bedrooms upstairs and one bathroom. I was to have one bedroom, my parents another bedroom, and Gertrude was to have the third bedroom.

My father (a.k.a. John Barrymore)
and his mother-in-law Gertrude

Soon after buying the house, my father established his own little electrical contracting business. "Syme's Electric—Residential, Commercial, Industrial Wiring. No Job Too Big or Too Small." His office was at the back of the house, and the garage served as his storage shed. He bought a used red Ford one-half-ton panel truck with a ladder rack on the roof, and he was ready to do business.

Gertrude sold the Dauphin home and moved into her little room on Cathedral Avenue. It was a disaster from the start. She hadn't lived in such primitive quarters for many years. There were no maids to help out. She didn't trust Bob the playboy. She was still angry with Rose for behaving foolishly. I never was able to find out why she left Dauphin in the first place. Her sons, Harry and Saul, were there. Why didn't she move in with them? Was Bob that persuasive? In any case, it was a bad decision and she didn't stay in that little room for long. The boys in Dauphin kicked in money that allowed Gertrude to rent a small apartment one block down the street on Cathedral Avenue. My mother later in her life reported that this move was a relief for all.

5

EARLY YEARS IN WINNIPEG: FIDDLER ON THE ROOF REVISITED

My memory of the North End in Winnipeg is that of a battlefield. I remember the Ukrainian kids hunting down the Jewish kids every day as if they were conducting a pogrom back in the old country. As I was writing these words, I wondered how the old neighborhood is described today, and I looked it up on Wikipedia:

"The North End: Bounded by Inkster Boulevard to the north, McPhillips Street to the west, the Red River to the east and the Canadian Pacific rail tracks to the south in Winnipeg, Manitoba. The North End has a long history of drug and gang violence within its boundaries, and is also a diverse neighborhood. Gangs such as Indian Posse, Native Syndicate and Manitoba Warriors are based in this area. 78,000 residents live in this area. It is the largest Ukrainian centre outside of Ukraine itself."

It hasn't changed much in the sixty years since I was there. In the old days, it was a working class neighborhood. But it was a working class neighborhood with a difference. Typically, working class people live in one area of town, and wealthier people live in other neighborhoods. Not in Winnipeg. The Jewish people were not permitted to live in the better parts of town regardless of their wealth. This is one classic definition of a ghetto—a section of a city where all Jews were required to live, regardless of income. I clearly remember my parents and other adults talking about their "ship coming in" and being able, one day, to live in River Heights. Hah! The River Heights neighborhood was out of the question in those days. As was true in the Ukraine in the nineteenth century, Jews in many parts of Canada were still required to live in a ghetto. This discrimination existed in many aspects of living as well. I recall discussions with my friends about strategies for applying to medical schools or law schools. I recall Morris Silverman saying to Allan Decter, "Why do you keep talking about getting into McGill University Medical School? They only take five Jewish kids a year and you'll never make it." And Larry Katz telling Sam Herman, "You'd be better off applying to the Alberta law school than the Manitoba one because they don't have many Jews applying and you'd have a better chance."

As a result of these restrictions about where Jews could live, my street, Cathedral Avenue, included working class families as well as very wealthy families, all in one block. The Sheps family, for example, lived across the street, a few doors down from our house but their house was fancy and enormous. They owned a large insurance company in town. The Fertigs lived four doors down the street from our house. They were furriers and they owned the largest fur shop in Winnipeg. Fur shops, as you can imagine, were big business in the frozen tundra of Manitoba! Their house was also very big and impressive. There were middle class families as well on Cathedral Avenue. The Silverbergs lived six doors down. Jack Silverberg was a mathematics teacher at the high school and later became a principal. The Adelman family lived nine houses away. Mr. Adelman owned two movie theaters in town. Their two sons enter my story later on in a very important, and corrosive, way.

I mention all this because this ghetto battlefield became a central driving force in my life and in the life of my friends. Let me explain. Despite the fact that all the Jews in Winnipeg, rich and poor, were forced to live in the North End, they were still far outnumbered by non-Jewish Ukrainians who brought their anti-Semitism with them from Europe when they migrated. Both groups attended an undistinguished elementary school. Champlain Elementary School was one block from my house but it felt like miles. My friends and I learned to travel this long, treacherous distance to the school in devious and clever ways so as to avoid attacks by the Ukrainian kids in the neighborhood. They knew our routes so we were always devising new ways of confusing them. We succeeded about 90 percent of the time. Not bad, considering.

The Ukrainians were clearly the majority group in the North End. Nothing I say about them can be taken as fact. They were the overwhelming and damaging presence in my childhood and, to this day, I still have a visceral reaction when I hear a Ukrainian name. There is an excellent Canadian Broadcasting Corporation reporter, Dan Karpenchuk, obviously a Ukrainian, who occasionally provides commentary on my National Public Radio station regarding events in Canada. When I hear his name on my car radio, my heart always skips a beat and I need to pay extra attention to my driving.

After surviving six years at Champlain Elementary School, I was promoted to Machray Middle School. I was older, and craftier, and could run faster, but the route to this school was also much longer and far more treacherous. It was a half mile away. There were no school buses in the North End and we had to walk to this school in driving snowstorms with Ukrainian kids lurking all along the way. Our escape success rate was now down to about 80 percent. Still not bad. But exhausting.

My friends and I eventually graduated to St. Johns Technical High School in the North End of the city. The overwhelming majority of students in that school, mostly Ukrainians, spent most of their time in wood or metal shops. They were learning one or another manual trade, as befits a working class neighborhood. It was not a very good school. My friends and I were in what was called the "college preparation" track. We studied Latin, algebra, and English literature. Almost all of us in that class were children of first or second-generation Jewish immigrants. I always thought of our group as a "huddled mass." We really seemed a modern-day, Canadian version of the persecuted people in *Fiddler on the Roof.* This was a sad and ironic reality. Almost all of the older Jews in Winnipeg (and in Manitoba for that matter) had fled the pogroms of the Ukraine at the turn of the century. And here they were, after hopefully and optimistically traveling in very primitive conditions for thousands of miles to the new promised land, surrounded by the very people from whom they were trying to escape! In Winnipeg in the 1940s, we experienced a more civilized (but not much) continuation of the old Ukraine hostility. It still doesn't seem fair to me.

This unfairness became a guiding light for the rest of my life. Talk about transformative revelations! Many lights went on in my head. I had to figure out a way to escape this persecution. Gertrude, my grandmother and herself an escapee from the Ukrainian wars in the old country, made it very clear to me that the only way to survive the modern-day war with the Ukrainian thugs was to "get an education" so that you could then leave the battlefield once and for all. All my friends at St. Johns had received the same advice, and we all studied Latin declensions as if our survival depended on it.

The other advice we all got was to "hang a shingle" when we grew up. Gertrude used to say, "You need to be a professional of some kind—a doctor, a dentist, a lawyer, an accountant. Then you can be in business for yourself." What she meant was "Don't rely on others to give you a job. They won't. You need to be on your own!" The background for this advice was based on our collective grandmothers' conviction that Jews could never count on others and that you needed to be independent. I recall challenging my grandmother about her old-fashioned thinking: "The world is not like it used to be, Grandma. Those days are over." I remember her saying, "We used to think that way too, but your so-called gentile friends can turn on you in one minute if things get bad. I have seen it happen."

In spite of these warnings, I was not a very good student. Better than average, perhaps, but I was not in the same league as Jack and Joe Adelman. They were nonidentical twins who, as I mentioned, lived nine houses away from me when they (unknowingly) ruined my entire school career in Winnipeg. No matter how hard I studied, they always got better grades than I did. And I really did study. All of my friends would gather at the local soda shop ("The It") on Main Street on Friday night while I stayed at home doing my homework. As far as I could tell, neither of the Adelman boys did any homework at all. It was very frustrating for me. I still think about this injustice from time to time, even now as an old emeritus professor. Jack became a judge in the New York Supreme Court and Joe was a vice president at one of the Hollywood studios. I re-met Joe a few years ago in California, and I was still resentful of the unfairness of it all. I'm sure he wondered why I looked at him in such a hostile way. The perceived unfairnesses were piling up. The Ukrainians following the persecuted Jews to the new land. The Adelman twins getting good grades even though (in my jaundiced view) they didn't work hard. Not fair.

The persecution that my friends and I experienced every day in the North End seemed to be a driving force for all of us. Most of my friends from those days were successfully able to function in a world beyond the North End. Marvin Reynes lived with his family in a little shack behind his father's corner grocery. His family was poorer than mine, and his parents were even less helpful than mine. He ended up as a highly respected obstetrician/gynecologist in Los Angeles. Allan Decter was the son of a Winnipeg bus driver. He ended up as one of only two pediatric urology surgeons in Canada. He was world famous for his brilliant and intricate surgery on genetically malformed sexual organs in infants. Sam Muchnick, the son of a salesman, ended up a distinguished dental surgeon. Sid Kahana, the son of a bank clerk, ended up as a nuclear physicist of some renown. Larry Katz, the son of another salesman, ended up in Los Angeles as a wealthy supplier of motel furniture. Sam Herman, son of a mechanic, became an architect. And as I mentioned earlier my nemeses, Jack and Joe Adelman, ended up on the New York Supreme Court and as a vice president of 20th Century Fox movie studios, respectively. When I recently told my daughter this story of achievement, she said there must have been something in the water back then. The fact is, it wasn't the water. It was a fear of being condemned forever to being beaten up on a daily basis. However, I am not recommending this as a strategy to motivate children to study hard.

Other children from the North End—older, and not of my generation—did well too. Gertrude's brother, Alter Cherniack, was a distinguished lawyer and community leader who founded one of the first independent Jewish Studies Schools in North America. His son, Saul Cherniack, also a lawyer, served in the Manitoba Assembly for nineteen years and, as a cabinet member during some of those years, amalgamated the suburbs of Winnipeg with the inner city to form one large municipality. This was the first such unification in North America. In 1985, he received the Order of Canada—the highest honor granted by the Canadian Government on behalf of the Queen of England. And as I noted earlier, Max and Ann Goffman's son, Erving, became a famous man. After leaving Dauphin and the North End of Winnipeg, he became one of the most famous sociologists in the world. He was a professor of anthropology and sociology at the University of Chicago, at the University of California at Berkeley, and finally, at the University of Pennsylvania. He wrote many outstanding books, but the book that launched his career and that is still a classic is the first one he wrote in 1959: *Presentation of Self in Everyday Life.* (It still sells briskly at Amazon.com.) Whether or not Erving's parents ever read it, I don't know. But the book is a veiled criticism of his crude millionaire father Max and his status-conscious, keep-up-with-the-Joneses mother, Anne, living in their very expensive house with sweeping cypress trees overlooking the Red River.

One of the sons in the Sheps family across the street from my house on Cathedral Avenue also became an important and influential man. After leaving Winnipeg, Dr. Cecil Sheps became the director of the Beth Israel Hospitals in New York and Boston and later became professor of Social Medicine and Epidemiology, as well as a vice chancellor for Health Affairs, at the University of North Carolina. In 1991, the university renamed its health center in his honor.

6

MY FATHER: BAD GUY OR PARAGON?

It is probably too simplistic to claim that growing up in the Winnipeg battlefield explains success in later life. One can be motivated to get out of the line of fire but that doesn't mean that one can be successful in doing so. One probably needs a role model as well. Or other resources, guidance and help. The reason that I am so interested in my situation is that I had no role models or guidance or encouragement, and I think that poses an interesting puzzle.

Earlier in this accounting, I mentioned two family members who had gone to universities and did well. Were they not role models for me? Chuck Bay was a brilliant man who got his masters of business administration at Harvard University and went on to have an amazingly successful career as a businessman. He was vice president of the Bonwit Teller Department Store in New York when, at the young age of forty, he had a massive heart attack and was forced to lead a less high-profile life from that time on. (Despite this premature medical crisis, he died at the ripe old age of eighty-three.)

Erving Goffman, as I have mentioned, was a very successful scholar. Unfortunately, both of these people fled the Winnipeg scene as soon as they were able and neither was part of my life in Winnipeg. I knew about them, of course, but I was not able to identify with either.

I perhaps need to say a little more about the influence that my father had on my life. I have already described his conclusion that I was useless. He put me down whenever possible. But he was not simply a bad guy. He also was a very hardworking man. He worked hard all day at the telephone company and then worked every evening and weekend studying to get his electrical contractor's license. He bought an old house and worked tirelessly to remodel it. He invited his mother-in-law to come live with him. He had high standards for the work he did, and he expected others to honor those standards as well. Clearly, he was a complex person.

I am unable to provide an objective description of him because of the struggles I have had to overcome the "useless" label he branded me with. How to be fair and objective? I sought my daughter's thoughts about this. Karen is a marriage and family therapist who is extraordinarily skilled in sorting through these kinds of complexities. I described to her my problem in summarizing my father's strengths and weaknesses, and after quietly listening to my confused ramblings, she said, "Your father didn't feel he was a good enough man." Bingo. That insight, I think, explains a lot of his behavior. My father grew up in a poor family with hardworking but unsupportive parents. Yet that family produced two extraordinarily successful sons of national renown. One was a lawyer. The other was a rabbi. And both were famous and accomplished. My father dropped out of school at the end of eighth grade. His brothers were articulate, and my father was not. The way that my father rationalized all this was to say that he had taken jobs so that he could contribute to the education of his brothers. Without his help, he said, they wouldn't have been able to do what they did. So instead of him being left behind by his brothers, he was able to claim partnership with them. Whether his story was true or not, I have not been able to ascertain. But that story was a way for him to maintain a certain comfort level with a situation that otherwise could have been very troublesome.

The reason that I question his story about helping his brothers is that my father rarely told the truth about anything. He always put a better spin on stories so that he looked better than he would otherwise be. For example, I heard him tell many prospective customers that he had dozens of employees in his company and that he had five trucks. In reality, he rarely had more than one employee, usually none, and he had only one truck. He wanted people to think better of him. The fact that I overheard him tell these exaggerated stories may have been awkward for him, and that may be yet another reason for him to put me down. On the other hand, I'm not sure he was even aware of his exaggerations. I sometimes had the feeling that he had come to actually believe his stories. He told them often enough.

I use the word "exaggeration" rather the word "lying." "Lying" is a nasty word. It is not telling the truth. Exaggeration, on the other hand, is an understandable stretching of the truth. It is portraying something as better than it really is. And this is a useful—but sad—strategy for a man who felt not good enough.

Feeling not good enough sheds some light on other things I never understood about my dad. When my mother and father went out to a party at friend's homes, he would always get dressed in beautiful and stylish clothes while my mother would be nicely, but plainly, dressed. He was the colorful peacock. To prepare himself for that evening's performance, he would always have two or three shots of Seagram's Crown Royal whiskey (the whiskey that Sam Bronfman made that comes in a purple velvet sac) before he left the house. And to ensure a consistently high level of performance during the evening, he would continue to drink all evening. He was the life of the party. He sang, danced, told jokes, and was the center of all attention. My mother never touched alcohol. She would sit quietly during these parties while her husband happily entertained everyone.

My daughter told me that people who do not feel good enough about themselves can end up resorting to alcohol and abusive behavior. I have already mentioned my father's abuse because of my sloppy work with screws and my small shoulders and my inability to crush bottle caps. But it went further than that. Every time I brought a young lady to meet my parents, my dad would inevitably take over. He would take her aside and regale her with his stories and cleverness. The message was clear to me: why are you hanging around with my useless son when you can see that I am much more lively and attractive and wonderful? Needless to say, I didn't bring young ladies around very much.

It is difficult to say whether or not my father was a liar. For example, I wonder how an observer would judge this situation? One time, in the middle of a cold winter night, my father received a call from a man saying that his furnace was not working. He had three children in the house. As I have mentioned, Winnipeg winters get very cold and not having a working furnace is a very dangerous situation. Would my dad come immediately to fix the furnace? My dad woke me to come with him. We arrived at the man's house to learn that his furnace had stopped working at three o'clock that afternoon and that he had already called upon four other different workmen try to fix it. Without success. My dad sent me out to the truck to bring in a ladder and tools while he went down into the basement to examine this very difficult and challenging problem. When I arrived in the basement with the ladder, he whispered to me, "The problem has nothing to do with the furnace. The problem," he said, "is in that electrical junction box underneath the stairs." He climbed up the ladder to examine the box, and sure enough, he was right. He was really a talented diagnostician. He could figure out what was wrong with almost any mechanical device without ever resorting to silly things like user manuals or instructions.

He then got down from the ladder and whispered, "Bring in lots of other equipment from the truck and keep going back to the truck until I tell you to stop." He explained that he could fix the electrical problem in a minute or two but that he needed it to look like it was a much more difficult and complicated job. This was because he needed to charge the man an outrageous fee for coming out in the middle of the night. He didn't want the man to feel cheated for having to pay this fee for a few minutes' work. "Let's make him feel the fee is worth it." Lying? Or making things look better than they were?

Whether or not he was a liar, I certainly was trained to lie. From my earliest days of his electrical contracting business, I was instructed to tell lies. On more occasions than I can count, I recall answering his business telephone—the office was located in the breakfast nook of the kitchen—and being asked to tell whoever was calling "I'm sorry, Bob is not here right now." This happened while Bob was sitting directly in front of me. The callers almost always were angry about something. "He said he would be at my house two days ago and he still hasn't come. What's going on?" "He said he was going to send me a check two weeks ago and I still don't have it!" "If he doesn't contact me today, I'm finding another electrician!" My father would sit in front of me with his fingers to his lips. I remember this telephone trauma to this day.

Why were things so out of control in my father's life? I think he took on projects and made promises that were totally appropriate for a man with many employees and five trucks. I think he really thought of himself in that way. He wasn't really lying. He could not deal easily with the fact that he was a very small businessman who was just getting by, one job at a time. He never felt good enough and he tried in every way he could to remedy this situation. This was the man who came to Dauphin and presented himself to Rose as a wonderful, successful, man of the world who could slay any dragons that came his way. This was the man who dressed as if he were ready to take his place in the latest movie production.

Having said all this, my father worked very hard to support his family. He rarely took vacations, he often worked on jobs all weekend, and he was always fixing something in the house. He built a large "social room" at the back of the house doing much of the work himself. He kept the small garage that came with the house but added next to it an enormous double garage with a big attic to better store his equipment. He did a lot of the work on that himself. He found a way to invite his mother-in-law to stay with us. For a man who was handicapped in so many ways, he certainly was able to accomplish a good deal. He was a complicated guy. And he never felt good enough about himself. It was too bad he felt burdened by a useless son as well.

What was the influence of this complicated guy on me? I learned many lessons that have guided my behavior ever since those days. I learned never to lie. And I find it excruciating to hear others tell lies. I shiver even as I type these words. I learned that I am a very poor workman. I hardly ever use a screwdriver, preferring to hire others to help me, even for the simplest of jobs. My handyman, Gifford Teeples, is always puzzled when I summon him to do a job any child could do. Perhaps some children can do that job, but not this child! I learned to work harder than most people to avoid confirming my father's label of uselessness. I learned about the importance of doing a good job. I learned about the importance of being an honorable man.

7

THE CORONATION OF A PRINCE

I feel I must address the issue of why I simply didn't accept my father's picture of me: I'm useless. Accept that view, go home, and relax. Here is what I think happened. I think I came to view myself as a really special young man. A young man who was loved, even adored, by many, many people. I know this a weird thing to say, but I recognize the feelings I used to have as a kid when I watch TV coverage of the President of the United States when he enters a hall. Surely you have seen those events where the president comes in and the band plays his presidential music ("Hail to the Chief!") and everyone stands and claps their hands and he goes into the crowd and shakes hands with a chosen few? That was me as a kid outside my home. I know that sounds somewhat grandiose, but let me put it in context.

Rose and Bob were the first children in either of their families to get married, and I was the first baby born in either family. I was, in fact, the first grandson. And as I have mentioned, when I wasn't crying, I was really cute. I also had a large group of relatives and family friends both in Dauphin and in Winnipeg. In Dauphin, my grandparents, Gertrude and Eli Bay, thought

I was wonderful, as did my uncles Saul and Harry. I was always also taken to see the Goffman and Buckwold families on my visits to Dauphin. My arrival in Dauphin was a special occasion. A cause for celebration. In Winnipeg, I visited my father's parent's home frequently where I spent time with Max and Anne as well as my father's sisters, Rose and Estelle. Rose had two children but Estelle had none. Estelle treated me as a wonderful gift. Also in Winnipeg were two of Gertrude's sisters who came to Winnipeg at the same time she did. Neither Anne Kimmel nor Rose Elkin was able to have children so I was very precious to them also. My mother had only occasionally engaged with these people earlier in her life but my arrival changed all that. She was still overwhelmed, shy, depressed, and quiet, but I at least caused her to leave the house and see other people. From all accounts, I was regarded as "a chosen one" by all of my relatives. Everywhere I was taken as a baby, I was greeted and fawned over. As a small child, I still recall being hoisted on countless shoulders and hugged by dozens and dozens of people. My cheeks were pinched to the point of pain. "Lennie is coming!" "Lennie is here!"

When I visited Dauphin, I recall going to Eli Bay Ltd. and being allowed to wander all over the store, without restriction. This was a big deal because Eli was a strict taskmaster and demanded that everyone behave in a predetermined and orderly manner. But not me. I had free rein. My favorite venue at Eli Bay was an X-ray-type machine that allowed you to see the bones in your feet. The purpose of the machine was to allow customers to see how well their new shoes fit. These machines have turned out to be a health hazard and they no longer exist anywhere. I am surprised I have survived this long after the countless hours I spent looking at my feet.

During the course of my days in the store, I would be introduced with enormous pride and joy to every customer that came in. Harry and Saul treated me as a special gift to the world. But their head salesman, Mickey, really celebrated my existence. Upon my entrance to the store he would run to greet me and raise me high above his head. In those days, Brylcreem was a favorite hair cream for men. Their slogan was "A little dab'll do you!" Mickey never got that message. He was a happy, cheerful, single man who learned Ukrainian and was the top salesman in the store. People would come by just to talk to Mickey. Mickey and I were great friends.

In the store (from the left): Uncle Saul,
Mickey the salesman, and Uncle Harry

On other days in Dauphin, I would visit the Buckwold's tractor store where I would sit for hours on bright green John Deere tractors and steer them through many imaginary fields and roadways. I was a terrific imaginary driver. People used to come by to ask my opinion about the tractor. And I think I must have generated lots of tractor sales for Jake and Alf Buckwold.

I recall also my time with Uncle Morris Elkin in Winnipeg. Since he and Aunt Rose had no children, they treated me with special attention and pleasure. Uncle Morris was a dour and humorless man who, I think, had been disappointed by everyone and everything in his life. I was his exception. I recall him taking me away to learn to drive a car. At the age of six. He would sit me on his lap and let me steer his old car and honk the old-fashioned claxon horn for hours on end. No one in the family had ever seen him behave so joyously and generously. That happy time with Uncle Morris was repeated in one fashion or another everywhere I went. I was the little prince.

As I have indicated, my father did his best to tear me down. My mother was a depressed woman who had lost her pleasure in living. But my extended family made up for all of this by the continual celebration of my life, no matter what I did, or did not do.

So even though I was never hugged at home, or sung to, or walked with, or read to, and even though my father was disappointed in me, I came away from all this with a good feeling about myself. As I have looked back on this, I think I felt that all the adoration and cheek-pinching from my extended family must be based on something! How could so many enthusiastic people be wrong? They must know something about me that I was not aware of! They must have known what they were talking about. I must be a special person.

My research, and the research of my colleagues in social epidemiology, has demonstrated that having good social connections is one of the most important factors of all in maintaining health. (A recent published paper reviewed 148 research studies among 300,000 people and found that having poor social connections was even more important than cigarette smoking as a risk factor for disease.) I now think that one of the reasons for this is that social connections help us understand, at some level, that we must be worthwhile people, and this, we know, has an important impact on biological functioning. So while good social connections are important for their instrumental and appraisal value, for the emotional support and comfort they provide, and for the possibility that financial help might be available, I now think that their importance for self-esteem should especially be emphasized: they can make us feel worthwhile as human beings and they therefore help us think that we can be wonderful and do wonderful things. I certainly felt that way about myself.

Looking back, I can see that my research has also been influenced, not only by an interest in social connections, but also by the idea of unfairness. While I was not conscious of it, my feelings about unfairness turned out to be an important guiding principle in my life. It has, in fact, been another major driving force in most of the work I have done. It has directed my thinking about the research I have chosen to do, about the students I have chosen to work with, about the people I have hired, about the budgets I have created over the years, and just about everything else I have done. In a way, my life has centered around this issue. I have always had strong feelings about the plight of people living in damaging circumstances, especially when those circumstances were not of their own making.

The central focus of work in social epidemiology is to better understand how social circumstances affect life chances and, subsequently, health, and well-being. The point of doing this research is to identify causal pathways so that interventions can be designed to improve the lives of people. All of my teaching and all of my research has centered around the importance of social support and around the identification and naming of unfairness. With Dr. Linda Neuhauser, I now am co-director of a center at Berkeley called Health Research for Action that is attempting to help people strengthen their social ties and confront and overcome the corrosive force of unfairness.

8

A BOY IN THE SALT MINES

When I wasn't studying super hard to keep up with the Adelman boys, I took as many paying jobs as I possibly could largely in order to repel my father's accusations of worthlessness. Someone was willing to pay me for my services. I worked very hard at these jobs every summer from the time I was twelve years old. Some of those jobs were well beyond my capabilities, but I worked at them furiously anyway. For example, I recall a job I had in a street construction crew one summer when I was fifteen years old. We were building Smithfield Avenue in a new suburban development in Winnipeg. The man in charge of the job was my Uncle Rube Kimmel. He owned a fairly large construction company in Winnipeg, and he was able to hire his young nephew to help out in the summer. My job was to negotiate a wheelbarrow to the back end of a large cement truck and wait until enough cement came down the chute to fill the wheelbarrow. Then I was supposed to roll the wheelbarrow down a long, narrow track of boards until I reached a designated spot where I was directed to tip it. The problem was that I was very young and I was really not strong enough to balance that heavily laden wheelbarrow on the narrow strip of boards. Too bad I had such narrow shoulders! If I allowed the wheelbarrow to tip over en route, it would be a major mess. It did tip, of course, several times, and it was, of course, a real mess.

I recall coming home during the first week of this job and going straight to my room to sleep. My mother said, "You look terrible! You're all dirty and you look worn out. Eat something!" I had worked a very long day and I must have been famished, but I know I was more exhausted than hungry and sleep won out. I should have quit that job but I didn't. I was not going to be seen as useless. By the end of that summer, I was bigger and stronger—physically, spiritually, and emotionally. Improving in those ways was of great importance to me later in life. I have always been a hard worker and have been willing to push wheelbarrows wherever they need to go.

I did the job with Rube Kimmel well enough that he hired me the next summer for another construction job. He said, "This time you won't have to push heavy wheelbarrows. Your mother was not very happy with me over that. This job is an easy one." And it was. This job was building a drive-in movie theater in Western Canada.

Many young people today might not even know what a drive-in movie theater is. Or if they know what it is, they certainly have never been to one. Richard Hollingshead built first drive-in theater in the world in 1933 in Camden, New Jersey. The trick that he figured out was to line up cars in an open field so that the car in front of you did not block your view of the very large movie screen that was placed off in the distance. He accomplished this feat by building little hills in the field that allowed the front wheels of your car to be elevated. Then all he had to do was build little posts next to each car that held a loudspeaker so the sounds of the movie could be heard in each car. The drive-in movie phenomenon then spread like wildfire. For fifty cents or so, one could bring the whole family to the movies. The kids could sleep in the car if they were tired. No babysitters needed. You could buy snacks and eat in the car. So one feature of the drive-in movie was that it provided cheap entertainment for the family. Another feature that quickly caught on was its value as a place for young couples to entertain themselves in a semiprivate setting.

Word of this new phenomenon eventually spread to Winnipeg and, in 1948, a drive-in theater was planned for North Kildonan, a suburb just outside the northern border of the North End. This was to be the first drive-in theater in Western Canada. While my job was going to be easy, the overall job was challenging because the little hills needed to be built in a very precise way. My job involved two tasks. First, I was to work with a surveyor to mark out the areas where the graders would carefully dump gravel to build the hills. Second, I was to direct hundreds and hundreds of loaded gravel trucks to place their loads in specific areas of the park and then sign their worksheets to acknowledge that they had done so. I worked long hours but this job was clearly within my competence. Except for one day.

One day, I was asked to get water to fill up a one-ton water truck. The truck was a beat-up old army water vehicle that was still painted army brown. It was the kind of truck that had spray nozzles attached at the back. The truck was used to spray water over newly deposited gravel as a dust control measure. Anyway, the truck needed water and the foreman said, "Kid, you can drive a truck, right?" I had never driven a truck in my life, let alone an enormous beast like that one, but I was sure I could figure it out. So I told the man "No problem!"

"OK," he said, "drive this truck down the main road for three miles and you'll see the Johnson Water Station on your right side. They know you're coming. They'll fill you up with water. Then get back here as soon as you can. We're waiting."

I was only sixteen years old and I did not yet have my driver's license. The truck was very big and it stood very high off the ground. I climbed a lot of steps and got into this monster. It had twelve forward gears and a very large steering wheel. But I found a way to move it. I drove it to the water station without incident and had the truck completely filled with water. Total success.

Then the adventure began. The truck was now very, very heavy. And I took a wrong turn leaving the water filling station and unfortunately ended up going down a narrow rural road away from the main street that I wanted to be on. Those who know me well can stop laughing now. I have always been directionally challenged. I used to think it was because I wasn't paying attention but I have recently learned that I have a brain defect! It's not my fault! I am disabled! This particular brain defect is located in the hippocampus adjacent to the dyslexia region of the brain (but it is not actually related to dyslexia). It's good to have a diagnosis because now I can look back at this episode and recognize that going down the wrong road was entirely understandable!

In any case, there I was driving down a very narrow road in an enormous, heavy truck. Going away from the drive-in theater, not toward it. That rural road seemed endless with no places to turn around. In desperation, I decided to turn around in the road anyway. I turned the steering wheel all the way (no power steering) and backed the truck up about six inches. Then, I turned the wheel all the way in the other direction and moved forward about six inches. And so on. During one of those backup maneuvers, I think I went further than the six inches I had intended, and the heavily laden truck began to slowly continue its backward motion. I, of course, immediately applied the brakes. But the truck was much too heavy for those little worn out brakes to contend with. And I just kept moving backward. Slowly. But surely. Until, finally, the truck settled into the roadside ditch, front wheels high in the air. And there I was. A trusted, hardworking young man with a lost truck and no water delivery for the job. There were no houses anywhere near my location, and it was about fifty-five years too soon for cell phones. Eventually, a car came down the road, took me to a farmhouse, and I was able to call a tow truck to get me out of my jam. I returned to the worksite without water and with a substantial towing fee.

While we are on the subject of water: During the spring of the disastrous Winnipeg flood in 1950, my friend Merv Silverman and I had a special, and dangerous, job. We rented two dozen sump pumps, and we started a business to keep basements dry. We had mostly residential customers but several business customers as well. Our job was to hook up the sump pumps, get them running when basements began to flood, and most importantly, maintain a constant vigil over them all day and all night during the two crucial weeks of overwhelmingly high water levels. That was the easy part. The hard part was driving a car, day and night, through badly flooded streets. We had to clamp a hose on the exhaust pipe of the car and attach the hose to the roof. The car's exhaust was now higher than the water level on the street. It was quite exciting navigating those streets so we could keep watch on our pumps.

Merv and I took turns napping, finding food, and repairing pumps. It was during those difficult days that I had my very first cup of coffee. In the middle of the night, the only food and drink that was available was from Red Cross volunteers. And the only provisions they offered were, of course, coffee and doughnuts. I had had a doughnut before, but this was my initiation into the adult world of coffee drinking. Merv and I made a lot of money during that time, but the money is not what drove me. Making money was a way of proving my usefulness in ways my father could understand.

I began working all of these jobs at an early age. My first summer job was to work for Pete Okopnick when I was twelve years old. He was the mild-mannered tailor I mentioned earlier. He married Rose, my father's sister. Pete had a little shop in downtown Winnipeg where, in addition to doing tailoring, he provided a "Press While You Wait" service. Businessmen would come to his shop, go into a little curtained booth, take off their suits, and have Pete press them while they waited in the booth. He hired me to take the suits from the men, run to him so that he could press them, and then run the suits back to the customer when the job was done. Speedy service was the advertised claim. I could easily handle most parts of that job. I had to take public transportation to and from the North End each day, on my own, but I could manage that. The challenging part of the job involved things I was not prepared for. First, summers in Winnipeg could be overwhelmingly hot with very high humidity. Running all day in a hot clothes-pressing shop was not such a good idea on those days. And those days occurred perhaps 80 percent of the time in the summer. There was no air-conditioning back then. To add to the fun, customers would often give me their suit and then say, "Hey, kid, for an extra ten cents, run across the street, and get me a Coke. And make it snappy." Pete was happy that I provided this special amenity for his customers. I would go home a worn-out boy most days.

An interesting addendum to this account about my jobs: My daughter read my account of these various jobs, and she knew that I got paid for my work. One day, she innocently asked me, "What did you do with all the money you earned?" I was stunned. I have no recollection at all about that. None. I have no recall about saving my money, or spending it, or giving it to my parents, or anything else. Zero. How is that possible? In retrospect, I think I hated the idea of having the money. I valued earning the money as a mark of my value, but I think I had no respect for the money itself. Another possible explanation is that I simply blocked out the money part from my memory. This apparently is not uncommon among abused people. But it is weird.

As you can perhaps see, I always had difficult jobs as a kid and I always worked as hard as possible all the time. No walking. Always running. Making sure the slots on the screws were carefully aligned. And while I worked and studied hard, I played sports hard too. I loved playing hockey, soccer, football, and especially baseball. My initiation into baseball occurred when I was ten years old, and I received a catcher's mitt as a gift from my Uncle Saul. I had very few toys as a child (Uncle Harry gave me a red Radio Flyer wagon when I was four years old) and that baseball mitt launched me into a mini career as a catcher. In those days, we played baseball with no other protective gear and that was particularly dangerous if you were a catcher. When I was knocked out the second time by a bone-numbing foul tip, I traded my catcher's mitt for a first baseman's glove and began to play that position. Much safer. I played all my sports with a fierce passion. I was not very good, but I certainly tried hard and gave it my all. Another form of pushing wheelbarrows.

That my father considered me useless had two important and long-lasting consequences for my life. One I have just described: I worked very hard in everything I did so as to prove him wrong. The other more unfortunate consequence has been that I have avoided getting involved in activities where I was likely to fail. "Fail," however, is a special word for me. A grade of "A" is acceptable. Anything less than that is a failure. It proves that I am indeed useless. From this perspective, it made sense for me to avoid challenges in which a grade of "B" or less was a likely outcome. As a life strategy, this means that many wonderful things in life have been unavailable to me. I am even now, at the age of seventy-nine, working very hard to learn that "average" and "moderate" are acceptable outcomes for my efforts.

Here, as an example, is one unfortunate consequence of my inability to accept a grade of less than "A." For several years in the very recent past, I spent all of July in Paris with a very special friend. She was brilliantly fluent in conversational French, but I was hopeless. In the evenings and weekends, when we were together, I remained silent while she ordered food in restaurants, bought movie tickets, and shopped in stores and in the open-air food markets. During weekdays, when she was at work, I would struggle to communicate by using hand signals and other futile gestures. I was dreadful. We could never go to a French-language movie together. One summer, I decided that this foolishness had gone on long enough and I enrolled in a conversational French class at the Alliance Française. It was quite expensive but, in my view, absolutely necessary.

I should point out that I can read French fairly well. When I was working on my Ph.D. at Yale, it was required that all candidates for that degree have a reading knowledge of two foreign languages. This requirement was based on an old-fashioned understanding that the best science was being done in Europe and that an American had better be prepared to read the foreign literature. That requirement has long since been abandoned but it was still an issue at Yale in those days long ago. I had studied French (and Latin!) in Winnipeg as a boy and was able to pass the French language-reading exam with little difficulty. I did spend a year at Yale studying German, and I was able to pass that reading exam as well.

Reading a language is one thing. Speaking it is an entirely different matter. I had never spoken French in my life.

The Alliance Française was five blocks from our apartment in Paris, and I set off each weekday morning at eight thirty to accomplish my goal. There were nineteen other students in my class, all of them young college students. I was the old man in the group. Some of the students came from the United States, others came from far-eastern countries, some from other European countries, and some from Latin America. Our teacher was a thirty-five-year-old man who was quite talented. He, of course, only spoke French to us. We worked together for four intensive hours Monday through Friday for the entire month of July. We were also given about three hours of homework each day. I studied very hard. I paid close attention in class and did all of my homework each day. And I was clearly the worst student in the class. Perhaps the worst student in the history of the class.

The teacher would come to class each morning and come directly to my chair and say "ca va?" I never uttered the expected "ca va bien" in return. I knew what the right answer was but I was not going to say those words and have everyone laugh at my pronunciation. I was a professor, after all, and I was not going to become an object of derision. The students in my class were going to have to find their humor in some other way. I sat silent for one, long, long month.

As anyone who has learned to speak a foreign language can attest, you cannot learn it without trying, without saying words and being corrected. It is a question of trial and error. It can't be done in any other way. But I was not going to get a grade less than an "A". Making mistakes might be OK for others, but it was not OK for me, the professor. I receive a grade of "A" or I do not play. Can you imagine a sadder story? Or a sillier story? But there it is. Another legacy of avoiding being seen as useless. As I have thought about this disaster, I came to an even sadder conclusion. I realized that I have avoided trying to do many things in my life if a grade of "A" was not guaranteed.

In my professional life, however, I always took chances. I began to work on topics that had never been studied before. I was doing pioneering work in my field. Before most other people. Wasn't that risky? Wasn't I putting my career and my reputation on the line? It is hard to explain this, but making a mistake in my research life has always been perfectly acceptable to me. I somehow think of those mistakes as something that is required to advance our understanding. I never have a problem with editors correcting my writing drafts or with colleagues pointing out that I got something wrong in my thinking. I welcome this help. In my professional world, I am on my own and out of my father's competence. He can't judge me because he knows nothing of my academic work. There is no way that he can say I am doing well or not doing well. I am out of his reach. Learning a language is a different matter. It is a more childlike activity and a failure in conquering this type of challenge puts me at risk of being criticized like when I was a child. I will avoid that at all costs.

9

BEING A GOOD BOY

Working hard was one way to prove my worth. Another way was to be a "good boy." I never felt free to be a rebellious teenager. I never argued with my parents. I always obeyed instructions and was unfailingly polite. I was a "good boy." To this day, when I see a child behaving as perfectly as I did, all my alarm bells go off, and I become very concerned for that child. A well-behaved child makes me very nervous.

One form of being a good boy was to obey my parents' instructions regarding my grandfather. My grandfather Max, my father's dad, had been a blacksmith all of his life. He was a short, very well-built, muscular man. He had spent so many years of his life holding a hammer that he could no longer straighten the fingers on his right hand. Those fingers were permanently bent, as if he was holding that hammer even when he wasn't. He was able to hold a piece of bread only if he held it between his thumb and forefinger. He learned his trade as a boy in the Ukraine, and the Manitoba Telephone Company was happy to employ him to put horseshoes on the horses that pulled the telephone company's wagons. When he retired at age sixty-five, he became very religious. He attended a very tiny, decrepit synagogue every day along with perhaps thirty-five other old, Jewish retired men. My parents had no interest in religion, but my father assigned me to attend the synagogue on Saturday mornings so that he would not have to. I was to keep his father happy. My children laugh when I tell them that, as an eleven-year-old boy, I had to walk the three miles to the synagogue every Saturday morning (no riding permitted on the Sabbath) in the blinding snow and frigid temperatures of a Winnipeg winter, uphill, both ways. While I exaggerated a little, it was a very difficult thing to do when temperatures were 40 below zero and when I had absolutely no interest whatsoever in religion. I was just being a good boy.

The synagogue was only perhaps twenty-five feet wide and fifty feet long. It had a balcony where women and children sat. The men were all old and they were all very religious. They went to the synagogue every day to pray. They took this very seriously. Some of them undoubtedly were able to speak English, but I only heard them speak Yiddish. When I would walk in on Saturday mornings, it caused a stir. The men would raise their heads from their prayer books and acknowledge my presence. That was it. But it was a big deal. I would then join my grandfather and pray with the men as if I knew what I was doing. I hated the whole operation but I was under orders, and I was nothing if not obedient.

As part of my effort to be a good boy, I worked hard to prepare for my bar mitzvah. From the time I was eight years old, I attended Hebrew school on Lansdowne Avenue every day after regular school. Every day, I would walk two miles (again, in the snow, against the wind, uphill both ways) to attend two hours in that school so that, at age thirteen, I would be able to stand in the synagogue and read the Torah. I attended this school with ten other boys, but I never socialized with any of them at any time. I was just doing my job. Fun was not part of it. I was very observant; every day, I would say my prayers and put on the phylacteries (small boxes with straps that were put on the forehead and arms). I did this so that, when questioned, I would get a grade of A. Shortly after I completed my bar mitzvah, I stopped all of these activities and never did any of them ever again. I did them only to please my grandfather (and, of course, indirectly, my father), but my heart was never in these activities. As an adult, I do not observe any Jewish holidays and I can't even remember their names or their significance. And I had no interest whatsoever in encouraging my children to be religious. So much for being a good boy.

Great-grandfather Eliahu Cherniack

I had another grandfather living in Winnipeg at that time. He was my great-grandfather. Gertrude's father. Eliahu

Cherniak. He was ninety years old at the time of my bar mitzvah. He lived in what we called an "old folks home" about four miles from my house in the North End. I used to visit him regularly as well. He was an intelligent, scholarly man who spoke a little English but who did not hear well. He had been principal of a highly respected Hebrew school in Winnipeg (the Talmud Torah) and was regarded by many as a "rabbi" without formal credentials. This honor was a tradition in the shtetls of Eastern Europe for wise men. It was difficult to talk to him because of his hearing problem, but I did my best. He was not nearly as religious as Max and he regarded religion as a tradition that was worth keeping but not as something that should take up much time.

When the date for my bar mitzvah approached, tension in the family increased. Should I have my bar mitzvah in the synagogue attached to the old folks home or in Max's little synagogue? Max really cared about this and wanted the event in his synagogue. I had been going there with Max for several years on a weekly basis, and shouldn't that count for something? It really mattered to him and his friends. Those on the Bay side of the family felt that Max's group was of a lower class. They were working men who spoke little English and who were poor and had little sophistication. Their synagogue was old and shabby and small. It soon became apparent, though, that their snobbish attitude was not enough to convince people to hold the ceremony at the old folks home. Max cared too deeply. Then members of the Bay family found a much more compelling argument. It was going to be very difficult, they said, to transport a frail, ninety-year-old man all the way to Max's place. Out of simple humanity, they said, my bar mitzvah should be held in the more convenient (and nicer) synagogue in the old folks home. So that was the decision.

Grandfather Max Syme

I was not involved in any of this fussing. I was madly preparing for the bar mitzvah ceremony that I didn't really care about. For those unaware, bar mitzvahs in those days were held only in the Hebrew language. Today, depending on whether the synagogue is Orthodox, Conservative, or Reform, the language can be in Hebrew or English. And depending on the same level of orthodoxy, women and children can sit with the men or be segregated into another room. And the place can be referred to as a synagogue or a temple. In my day, there was no choice: we all went to super-Orthodox synagogues where only Hebrew was read from the Torah and where Yiddish was the only spoken language and where women and children were condemned to the hinterland.

My Bar-Mitzvah
From the left: Grandmother Gertrude, mom, sister
Audrey, me, dad, grandfather Eliahu, Aunt Sonia
(wife of Rabbi Monte)

On the occasion of a bar mitzvah, the thirteen-year-old boy is welcomed into the company of men and is asked to read from the Torah as an induction ceremony. My sister sent me a little joke the other day that provides an alternative definition: It says that bar mitzvah is the day when a Jewish boy comes to the realization that he is more likely to own a professional sports team than he is to play for one. In those days, girls were never part of this ceremony. Today, girls have a bat mitzvah celebration at the age of either twelve or thirteen depending on the orthodoxy of the synagogue or temple.

In my case, six old men crowded around me as I began my recitation from the Torah. The men watched carefully to be sure that every word was pronounced properly. There are two problems that the bar mitzvah boy must contend with. These problems are the reason that a bar mitzvah boy spends three or four years preparing for the event. Reading normal Hebrew is difficult, but it can be done with some work. Reading Hebrew as it appears in the Torah is a different matter. In normal Hebrew, a letter appears along with little notations that tell you how to pronounce that letter. In the Torah, the same Hebrew letters appear, but they have no little notations. So the bar mitzvah boy must memorize the pronunciation of the multitude of words that will be read over a fifteen-minute interval. That is a lot of words. Then there is the matter of the melody. The words in the Torah must not only be spoken but they must also be sung, using the unwritten musical intonations passed down orally for thousands of years from elder to younger. Since there is no musical notation in the Torah, the music must also be memorized.

A large crowd attended my synagogue debut. All the folks from Dauphin came. Even my uncle Monte, the famous rabbi from Detroit, came. In fact, he led most of the service that morning. At the end of the ceremony, a dinner celebration was held at the Royal Alexandria Hotel. While the synagogue was filled in the morning, there was an even larger crowd at dinner. Perhaps a hundred people? At the dinner, I was expected to rise and make a speech thanking my family and everyone else for helping me to get to this point in my life. Then I received lots of gifts.

So this was a major life event. I have no idea where the money came to make it all happen, but it was an impressive day. Now comes the uncomfortable admission. I went through all the studying and reading and singing and speech-making, but I didn't care about any of it. The whole day was the creation of others. I did what was expected of me. I didn't care. I was just being a good boy. Judging from the congratulations I got from many of the people in attendance, I assume I did well. Of course, I did not receive any congratulations from my dad.

I had no idea how he felt about the day. And there was no comment from my mother either, because she didn't believe in outbursts of emotion.

Working hard was a way to prove my worth to my father. So I was a good boy but I was not happy about that. On the other hand, it was better than the alternative: to confirm that I was indeed useless. Here comes the result of all this: I learned to put aside my personal feelings. I did what was expected of me without engaging or feeling. Many years later, I went to a wonderful therapist, Dr. Sandra Goozee. Sandra asked me tell her about my life. Time after time, she would listen to my story and then say, "Well, Len, I have a clear picture of what happened, but I have no idea at all of how you feel about the things you are telling me." I was totally at a loss. "What?" I would say, "I have no idea what you are talking about!" I really didn't know what she meant. Feelings? What are they? Sandra said that feelings were things like angry, hurt, afraid, and happy. For weeks, my response to her continual harassment was "What? I don't understand." It took me months to finally begin to sense that I really did have feelings about the things that happened to me, and I finally begin to recognize that fact and to talk about it. I am still not very good at it, but I am much, much better than I used to be.

I was a good boy in many other ways beyond doing my bar mitzvah. I don't think I ever disagreed with my parents about anything. I don't think I ever raised my voice with them. I don't think I ever said no to them. I never confided in them either. I never asked their advice about anything. I was well-fed and well-clothed and well-housed, but I don't recall any expressions of love or happiness or warmth. Nothing of interest was ever discussed at the dinner table. I don't recall anyone saying, "So how was your day?" It was as if we were all on a treadmill doing the things we were supposed to do without emotion.

My father was busy putting on his show of greatness and my mother was going through the motions without engagement. And I was playing my part by being a good boy and not making any trouble.

Being a good boy even influenced the clothes I wore. I was well-clothed. I had nice clothes, but nothing I ever wore was of my choosing. When I needed clothes, I occasionally got whatever was available from the store in Dauphin (free!) or from one of several wholesale warehouses in Winnipeg. In the latter case, Saul or Harry would notify the warehouse owner that their nephew was coming to buy clothing. These warehouses would be closed on Saturday. But not for me. On a Saturday morning, after I had done my synagogue duties, my mother and I would drive (even on a Saturday!) to the Wholesale District, walk down an empty street, ring a bell on the outside, and wait for a large steel door to slowly open. Then the owner, typically a Jewish man from the Ukraine (my favorite man being Sam Nussbaum), would welcome us in. Oftentimes, there were no other customers in the place. This was a special favor for Saul's nephew. "What does the boy need?" the man would ask my mother. She might say, "He needs a sports jacket." Then the man would lead us down a long row in the cavernous building to a place where sports jackets could be found. There were usually hundreds and hundreds of sports jackets on hangers. But that was misleading. There might be three hundred brown houndstooth jackets on the rack, but all of them were in the same size. In my size, there might be only two different types of jackets. My choices were limited to whatever the man happened to have available that morning. "Tell the boy to pick one," he would say. I did what I was told. "Does the boy need anything else?" he would then ask. Welcome to the wholesale world.

There is an old Jewish joke that ends with the line "I can get it for you wholesale!" And everyone laughs. I don't laugh. Even when I am now offered wholesale prices as an adult, I turn around and head the other way. I therefore spend more money on clothes than I should by shopping in fancy department stores where they have more than one or two sports jackets to look at. They love me at Nordstrom. At that time in Winnipeg, however, I never protested or even discussed this matter. I was a good boy and I did what I was told. It probably wouldn't have helped to discuss this with my mother anyway. She would probably have said, "Oh, don't be silly! The prices here are wonderful!"

My sister Audrey has written a book about her experience in this family. She is seven years younger than I am, and she is a girl. She had a very different family experience than I did. But we had the same view of Mom. My sister's book is titled *Mom? Are You There? Things I Wanted to Discuss with My Mother*. Audrey's main point was that our mother was not present in the family. She was unemotional, found words of love awkward, and avoided physical affection. When my sister came to her in emotional pain, my mother would say things like "Pretend it doesn't bother you," or "Act like you don't care," or "Pretend it doesn't hurt." There was a lot of pretending going on. Authenticity was in short supply in my family.

On being a good boy: I recall one of my birthdays many years ago. My three children worked together to present me with a poster board full of my idiosyncratic sayings. One of those sayings was "There's corn to be eaten." This saying was based on the well-known fact that I always ate all the corn on the cob I was served at mealtimes. What my children discovered one day was that I do not like corn. They asked me, "Dad, if you don't like corn, why do you eat it?" I said, "Because there is corn to be eaten." Their astonished faces told the story. They did not understand that I was a good boy and that I ate what I was served. The fact that they memorialized my statement on the poster board was to emphasize that I was a very weird person indeed.

I now look back on my commitment to always "be a good boy" as a well-intended but misguided strategy. I am much better now in recognizing my feelings about "being good" but I still have a long way to go. I occasionally take on assignments in which I have no interest. I sometimes accept invitations to travel and speak when I really don't want to. My calendar is packed with meetings and trips and jobs, some of which I really don't care about. But what choice do I have? What would happen if I turned down some of these invitations? I guess I still fear that I wouldn't be loved anymore and my father would be proved right after all. One day, when I grow up, I'm going to say no to these inducements. Fortunately, most of the things I do are things I really am passionate about. Thank goodness for that.

10

THE GIFT OF ANDREW CARNEGIE

So there I was in Winnipeg being beaten up by other kids and being warned by my grandmother that those beatings were my fate for life unless I could get an education, a shingle, and escape. I had no encouragement or help regarding education from my parents. A few people in my extended family had gone to a University but they all lived elsewhere during my youth and they were not part of my early life. My father was proud of the fact that he had gotten along quite well with an eighth-grade education, and he was convinced that you could learn more from the "school of hard knocks" than from fancy books. Other than schoolbooks, there were no books in my house anyway. And there were never any discussions about events of the day or about ideas. My dad didn't care about these things, and my mother had checked out. I recall very clearly coming home all excited from school one day and, at the dinner table, telling my parents about an amazing fact I had learned at school that day. "Mom and Dad," I said, "do you know that when a light beam hits water, the beam is refracted so that when you look at an object in water, it really isn't where you think it is. It just looks like it's there!" My parents looked at me as if I was from Mars. My mom told me to eat my soup and be quiet.

As a child, I was not taken to interesting places to stimulate my imagination and I had no role models. In spite of my teacher telling me about the refraction of light, I think of none of my teachers as being inspirational. They were all stuck in a very tough part of town and they were trying to train kids as best they could. Their goal, I think, was to help us avoid future unemployment.

My personal salvation was the small neighborhood library two blocks from my house. The St. John's Library at 500 Salter Street. The library had a small brass plaque at the front door saying that Andrew Carnegie had provided funds in 1915 for its construction. I almost lived in that library, and by the time I left Winnipeg, I probably had read all, or most, of the library's collection. Fiction. Nonfiction. History. Adventure. Science. Many people refer to Carnegie as one of the "bad guys" in American history; he is criticized as being one of the "robber barons." To me, he was a hero and lifesaver.

How could a robber baron be a "good guy"? I actually did a lot of reading on the topic, and I found it quite interesting. The so-called "Robber Barons" were Americans who became the pioneer industrialists of the world. They earned their fortunes through coal, oil, iron, and the industries that depended on these products. The rise of these U.S. industries made America's economy the biggest and strongest in the world. But the incredible wealth and mansions amassed by these men was achieved at the expense of their workers who were poorly paid and who worked long, hard hours, oftentimes in unsafe conditions. This was the reason that they became known as "Robber Barons." They were cruel taskmasters. In addition to Carnegie, the list of other robber barons included John D. Rockefeller, Cornelius Vanderbilt, and J. P. Morgan.

I paid special attention to Andrew Carnegie, my hero. He was born in Scotland in 1835. He emigrated from Scotland with his parents and later became one of the world's richest men. His rise to power in the manufacture and sale of steel forever changed the way in which industrial production was organized in America. His U. S. Steel Company ruled the steel industry by using "vertical integration." This means, I learned, that he owned most of the industries that supported his steel industry (iron ore, other critical minerals such as coke, and the railroad). As a result, he paid less to make his steel and was able to sell it for less. Since he didn't pay his workers much money, they often organized for better pay and working conditions. His response was to lock them out and replace them. He also had "hired guns" (men from Pinkerton's Security Company) to intimidate the workers. These strategies stopped organized labor from developing in the United States for many years. He was not a nice man.

But here is the puzzle: while Andrew Carnegie was robbing and pillaging, he also made a commitment to build libraries in neighborhoods all over the world. He built 125 of them in Canada between the years 1883 and 1929! He also built 1,689 libraries in the United States, 660 in Britain and Ireland, and others in Australia, New Zealand, Serbia, the Caribbean, and Fiji. So while some people called him the Robber Baron, others called him the Patron Saint of Libraries. Very few towns that requested a grant, and that agreed to his terms, were refused a library.

As I did research on this, I learned that in the early twentieth century, a Carnegie library was often the most imposing structure in hundreds of small communities all over North America. I always knew that my little library in Winnipeg had a unique architectural style, but I learned later that most of the library buildings he funded were unique. I learned that members of each chosen community were encouraged to pick the architectural style that they thought was most appropriate for their town. Styles available ranged from Beaux-Arts, Italian Renaissance, Baroque, Classical Revival, to Spanish Colonial. Most of his libraries were classic and formal. They were all designed to welcome people to the building by having them first climb a stairway, enter through a large and prominent doorway, and then climb up a second interior stairway. In the St. John's Library in the North End, the second interior stairway offered a choice of coming up one of *two* long curved staircases! A man I recently interviewed about these libraries said that the entry staircases symbolized a person's elevation by learning. There was also a lamppost outside my library to symbolize enlightenment. My library featured dark oak woodwork and beautiful antique reading tables. There was nothing else in the North End that came close to this building in magnificence or, to me, in importance.

The story of Andrew Carnegie presents a set of challenging ethical and moral issues. On the one hand, he was a brutal and cruel businessman; on the other hand, he was a magnificent philanthropist who improved the lives of many people all over the world. People often cite the story of Alfred Nobel as another man who was evil in one part of his life but a great man in another part. I disagree with this interpretation of Nobel's contributions. It is true that he was a co-developer of dynamite, but his intention in doing that was to see how to put this creation to practical use in construction work. Nobel realized that the safety problems associated with nitroglycerine had to be solved and that a method needed to be developed for its controlled detonation. Other people later misused his work, but he was clearly a good guy who wanted to help. That he left his fortune to establish the Nobel Prize merely adds to his distinction. Bill Gates provides another, more contemporary case. Gates was a ruthless and cruel competitor in developing Microsoft and he ended as one of the richest men in the world. The Bill and Melinda Gates Foundation, however, is now doing wonderful work all over the world in helping improve the plight of impoverished people. I have no answer to the ethical problem posed by these stories. I am obviously grateful to Andrew Carnegie, but I can understand that others would not be. This can be a great topic for college students to debate in the coffee shop.

I visited the Carnegie library on a recent trip back to the North End. It was a pilgrimage. The rest of the neighborhood had aged noticeably, but the library was still perfect. Shiny and beautiful. I was there in the middle of a weekday and the place was filled! Mostly young people. The main difference was that half the people were now working on computers instead of reading books. While I am not one to reminisce about the good ol' days and bemoan all the complicated new technologies available to us, I did suffer a little pang of sadness that the role of books has diminished these days. I'm not sure that computers can take their place.

My visit to the Carnegie Library

On that recent trip to Winnipeg, my colleague Dr. Doug Jutte drove me to 274 Cathedral Avenue. Our old house is now one of the best-maintained houses on the street. While it is painted a garish and almost painfully bright blue color, it is clear that it is being lovingly cared for. The other houses on the street looked a little shabbier but they too are in reasonably good shape. The main difference I noticed is the large number of people of Asian descent (mostly Filipino) on the street. Manitoba has become a major attraction for immigrants in recent years. Unlike many places in the United States, Canada is trying to attract more immigrants. Canada does have the second largest landmass in the world, and it has always been a challenge to find people to occupy that land. As Manitobans will unhappily attest, however, most immigrants have a preference for "MTV"—Montreal, Toronto, and Vancouver.

Manitoba is always on the short end. Most immigrants that do end up in the more humble, frozen land of Manitoba have tended to be Chinese, Indian, and Filipino. There are now, in fact, four Filipino newspapers in the city as well as a large annual Hindu Diwali festival.

While Asians were now clearly in evidence, Jews were nowhere in sight. They had fled the North End and are now living in such previously forbidden neighborhoods as Tuxedo, River Heights, Kingston Crescent, Waverly Heights, and River Park. When I last visited Winnipeg, the mayor was an immigrant from Israel, Sam Katz. He was the first Jewish major of the city. In his election to this office, he defeated a Ukrainian, MaryAnn Mihychuk. Things have certainly changed in Winnipeg.

Why was the library so important to me? One answer might be that it provided a safe haven from the physical threats of the neighborhood hooligans. But the library also provided me a safe haven from the other, more hurtful, threats imposed by my father. I think I was trying to find a way of "being" in which I would be immune from my father's criticism and devastating judgments of my worth. In the library, I could deal with stories and ideas that he knew nothing about. There was no way he could say to me "You think that's a good idea? Let me tell you about a much better idea." Or "You liked that book? I've read many books much better than that!" I was safe in a world beyond his comprehension and immune from comparison with his achievements.

My life as an intellectual, born in my Carnegie library, saved me most of the time from my father's criticisms, but not always. I recall one day when I told him I just had my very first paper published in a professional journal. This paper was based on a writing assignment I was given in one of my classes when I was a doctoral student at Yale. The professor, Charles

Snyder, was impressed with my work and suggested I submit it for publication. It was the first time Professor Snyder had ever done that sort of thing. Many people have to wait years before they can get a paper published, and here I was succeeding in this achievement at the age of twenty-five! The paper was titled "Personality Characteristics and the Alcoholic: A Critique of Current Studies." It was published in the *Quarterly Journal of Studies on Alcohol.* I happened to mention this to my father when I was visiting him. That was a mistake. Instead of being impressed and congratulating me on my success, he said, "How much did the journal pay you for your paper?" I said, "Things don't work that way in the academic world, Dad. People don't get paid for their papers." He walked away as if I had once again failed in crushing the soda bottle cap.

In the early days, my father's assessment of me as worthless was devastating. And no matter how hard I tried, I could not seem to turn things around so that he would change his mind. His assessment left me we with several legacies. One legacy is that I am one of the hardest-working people I have ever met. At the age of seventy-nine, I still work in my office every day and at home on Saturdays and Sundays and in the evenings. Even now, it is difficult for me to lie around, doing nothing. A second legacy is that I feel I must do everything very, very well. I need to get an A grade in everything. A third legacy is that even good accomplishments are never enough. There are undoubtedly some screw slots, somewhere, that are not aligned!

11

THE CHALLENGE OF UPWARD
SOCIAL MOBILITY

M̲y grandmother's advice that I get an education so as to escape the North End had an important impact on me. However, the proclamation that I was a useless boy could easily have sabotaged any plans I might have had to escape. Fortunately, the "useless" label was softened by the adulation I received from other people in my family. They said I was a good person. The implication was that I could succeed in escaping. In addition, I couldn't be that useless since so many people were willing to pay me to do jobs for them. And the Carnegie library opened whole new worlds of opportunity for me that I never would have known about.

All that was fine. But it seems to me that even with all these things going for me, it was not enough. I think people from disadvantaged backgrounds need to know how to intelligently navigate the system if they hope to escape. To be upwardly mobile, a special kind of intelligence is needed. I do not consider myself to be particularly bright in the conventional sense. I was an above average student and I am perhaps an above average researcher, but as a professor at a top flight university, I meet faculty and students all of the time who are really bright and I know that I am not in their class. My three children are far brighter than I ever was. There are, however, several types of intelligence and I think I have good interpersonal intelligence. People with this type of intelligence are leaders among their peers, they are good at communicating their ideas, and they understand other people's feelings and motives. As a child, I was the leader of my group of peers. These friends shared with me their hopes, fears, and secrets, but I shared virtually nothing with them. I could always tell what was on their minds, but I doubt they ever could discern my thoughts.

Here is my thinking about this: I grew up with no guidelines about how to think or behave in the world of ideas. I sat in my library and read extensively and I was well aware that there was a larger, and more interesting, world out there. I had a fantasy that perhaps I could even be part of that world. But I had very few skills to help me move into that world. I exemplified the classic case of the upwardly mobile person: someone who is moving into a world for which he is not prepared. This kind of person has to learn how to do things appropriately: how to dress, how to use eating utensils, how to speak, how to sit, how to enter a room, and so on. I knew nothing about these things. So I learned to watch carefully and to really listen to what people were saying, and not saying. To observe what they did and did not do. I learned to be quiet so as to not give myself away. I thought that if you share your thoughts and fears, you become vulnerable and then all kinds of bad things can happen. Abraham Lincoln got it right: "'Tis better to be silent and be thought a fool, than to speak and remove all doubt."

I developed two strategies for survival. One, I became very skilled at diagnosing people and situations. Who I am talking to? What is his agenda? What is the problem that is really being addressed? What needs to be done? A second strategy was not to reveal the insights I was developing. Keep them to myself. I did both of these things as if my life depended on it. And in my view, it did. So I think I developed a special kind of interpersonal "intelligence" that allowed me to escape my origins. I have always been able effectively to enlist the help of others in accomplishing my purposes. My goal, however, is to not "use" people. I benefit from their help, of course, but they need to benefit as well. That is the secret, and I know it well. This is hard for many people to pull off, but it is not at all difficult for me. I can do it without much effort or thought. It is my way of being. My daughter Karen, the therapist, has pointed out that abused children often develop hypersensitivity regarding other people's feelings in order to keep themselves safe. That's me.

There was a time when I was chairman of a department in the School of Public Health. It was a very large and diverse department. It included a Division of Epidemiology, a Division of Biostatistics, a Division of Infectious Diseases, and a Division of Environmental Health Science. Being chairman of such a large department is a difficult job that most sensible people avoid. One of the main challenges is that the faculty members in these groups are very aggressive in protecting their turf. They are also very smart, independent, and not usually willing to acknowledge authority from above. They are a feisty, articulate, and independent group.

To do the job of chairing this bunch, I organized an Executive Advisory Committee that, under normal circumstances, would have included the chairs of each of these four divisions. But I knew that if I did that, each of these chairs would continuously fight with me, and each other, to get more of whatever was available to them. I couldn't face the fighting and anger that would inevitably ensue. I needed to be safe. I needed to not be challenged. I needed to more safely navigate this treacherous set of rapids and avoid the predictable trouble. My solution was to appoint only three of these chairs to the advisory committee with the promise that the missing fourth person would be asked to join as I regularly rotated membership on the committee. The consequence of this was that the three people could not argue for their division since the committee was obviously not representative of the department. As advisors to me, they would have to transcend their parochial roles and think about the good of the department. It would be unfair to argue for their division when one division was not represented at the table. This arrangement worked amazingly well, and I survived a seven-year term with few arguments, enemies, or turf wars. Everyone I worked with in those days is still my friend.

In other parts of my life, I continue to be very careful of where and how I walk and talk. I avoid situations and people where I know there is likely to be trouble. I do not write Letters to the Editor or join groups that are protesting things. I tend to lay low and stay out of trouble. I do this even though it is no longer necessary. I have succeeded in my mobility. I arrived many years ago. I know how to eat, dress, talk and behave. Why am I behaving as if I am just emerging from the North End?

I recall a meeting where my "hiding" was challenged in public. I had just given a talk before two hundred people in which I suggested the importance for health of the concept "control of destiny." At the end of my talk, Dr. Peter Schnall stood up and said, "Why are you pussyfooting around the real issue. You are talking about power! Why not say it?" I then explained, right there in public, that I had a tough early career in which talking about "power" to my medical colleagues was going to offend many people. It would sound as if I were a left-wing rabble-rouser! I had a hard enough time, I said, in even introducing the idea of social factors. But now that social factors were being accepted as important issues throughout the world, I asked myself, in public, why was I still so nervous? I told my audience that I didn't know the answer. It was an awkward moment.

I suppose old ways of being tend to persist long after they are necessary or useful. I am aware of this and am trying to do better. But I always have with me the question "What if I blow it and get a grade of B?"

In spite of my ducking and weaving to stay out of trouble, I have somehow managed to be an influential person. I do, carefully, express my opinions. My views are honored and respected by others. I am not hiding in the corner as much anymore. But I do pick the time and place to express myself, and I am careful to keep my eyes and ears open for danger. It's too bad to be burdened by all this at my age, but there it is.

12

MONEY: A COMPLICATED ISSUE

I need to say something about the importance of money in my life. When I was growing up, I recall my parents describing certain people as "doing very well." I learned over time that what they really meant was that these people were wealthy. In their worldview, making a lot of money meant that one was "doing well." I also recall actually meeting some of these people. One, for example, was financing the drive-in theater in the North Kildonan district that I described earlier. He was a man my parents had said was "doing very well." On a particular Monday morning, he showed up to inspect progress on our construction job. He was a terrible person. He was rude to everyone. He walked around criticizing all of us and finding fault with everything. In my opinion, he might have been a wealthy man, but he was not "doing very well" as a human being. I made many observations during my youth with regard to other people in Winnipeg whom my parents admired. I decided that money was not the measure of a man. Actually, I came to avoid the issue of money whenever I could because it seemed to overwhelm everything else important in life.

And yet I later on found myself working on many jobs to earn money and making an important decision about which university to attend based simply on money. I did those things but I always resented it. When I finally was in a position in life in which my survival was not dependent on money, I erased money from my consciousness and my daily life. In my adult life, for example, I have never asked about the salary of a job I was considering. I never asked for a promotion. I avoided budgets, and my mind went blank when people around me discussed them.

I have not yet introduced my wife, Marilyn. I will talk about her at length later on in this account. For now, however, let me say that Marilyn was a master of dealing with money, and that was probably the only reason I was able to survive. I was basically of no help to her or to our family. Marilyn, in fact, used to take the money available for a month's living and divide it into separate envelopes. One envelope was for rent, one for food, one for clothing, and so on. When an envelope was empty, no other spending for that category of activity was permitted.

While I was grateful for her careful management, I was very unhappy with this way of living. I found it excruciating. The "envelope strategy" characterized our early life together. Later on, as I progressed in my career, when Marilyn told me that we couldn't afford something, I would find another job or other source of income so that I wouldn't have to hear those words anymore. At one time, I had three children going to University at the same time! The expense was, of course, far, far beyond the salary of a college professor. Rather than discuss this and make appropriate and rational plans, I simply got additional research jobs. Then, the issue did not have to come up. To this day, I really do not know my retirement salary or how much things cost. I can look these things up, of course, and I do, but they are not part of my consciousness. "Doing well" is important to me, but I never include money in that calculation. Instead, doing well, in my thinking, is being fair, being truthful, and making a difference.

During the time that I was chairman of the large department, I was responsible for a very large budget. Each year, I needed to allocate money to the four divisions. I know that the responsible way to do that job was to have each division submit a budget request. These divisions should itemize their personnel needs, their anticipated expenses for teaching assistants, research support requirements, office supplies, and so on. I should then have reviewed their requests in light of the number of students they were teaching and the number of courses they planned to offer. I knew these things. The way I handled this responsibility, in fact, was alarming. Unbelievably, I divided my departmental budget into four equal parts and gave each division one fourth of the budget. I should have been sent to prison for dereliction of duty. But I just could not bring myself to do the detailed budget analysis that was required. My vision would blur, my mind would wander, and I would begin fidgeting uncontrollably. And I knew that if my allocations were not equal, the ensuing fighting and arguments between the division heads would drive me crazy.

I had a wonderful assistant in those days. I chose Inga Fivian because she was a whiz with budgets. I think I caused her sleepless nights. She would from time to time say, "Len, we really do need to sit down and go over the department budget." I remember those times as if they happened yesterday. She would from time to time bring in these enormous books with millions of numbers in columns, and she would show me this crisis and that crisis and suggest that I make important decisions to resolve them. Within minutes of her presentation, my mind would cloud over. At appropriate times, I would interrupt her and say, "Inga, in light of what you are showing me, what would you recommend I do?" I always agreed with her and thereby escaped having to deal with the issue. Fortunately, I picked well. Inga was a gem. But I should have been arrested! Over the years, as I increasingly came to realize the seriousness of my paralysis regarding money, I tried to avoid jobs that involved similar types of financial responsibility whenever I could. Or at minimum, I made sure that I hired someone mature and capable who could bail me out. This is not a very pretty picture, but life on Cathedral Avenue compellingly convinced me that money is the root of not good things.

13

OXFORD IN THE PRAIRIES

I have discussed several factors that might explain how I was able to move from a nonintellectual life in a small Canadian prairie town to a more interesting life as a scholar at a major research university. These factors were dealing with Ukrainian oppression, working hard to confirm my worth, being a good boy, reading voraciously in my library, appreciating my princehood, and using my interpersonal savvy. Whether or not all of these factors were equally important and necessary, I cannot say, but my sense is, they are. My feeling is that if even one of these attributes had been missing, I would not have made it out of the North End.

In any case, I escaped. I finished my time at St. John's Technical High School and, at the age of seventeen, went on to the University of Manitoba. In those days, in Canada, there were twelve grades in high school, but those students who were college-bound could skip grade 12 and go instead directly to a freshman year at the university. There was no question in my mind that I would go to the university. All my friends felt the same way, and we all made the long, daily journey to the Fort Garry district where the university was then located.

By 1949, the university had recently expanded enormously to accommodate servicemen returning from the Second World War, and it now had an enrollment of 6,500 students. The university first started on the Fort Garry site in 1912 with six professors and one building. Today, it has an enrollment of 26,000 students in 60 buildings. The university now also has a health sciences complex in downtown Winnipeg with an additional ten buildings.

Me, age 17, Cathedral Avenue

The original Fort Garry site during my time there was a beautiful place located near the Red River. You will perhaps recall my earlier description of the Red River during springtime in Winnipeg and you can perhaps anticipate this next sentence. In the spring of 1950, when I was finishing my second year of college, the Red River overflowed its banks once again and the campus was totally inundated. Rescue and maintenance workers had to paddle around the campus in boats to help people and look after important equipment. The graduation ceremony was cancelled that year. The graduates of that year were forever after referred to as "the flood class."

When I began to study at the university, it was still very small and it offered a very narrow range of courses. There was no such thing as a "major." Like almost all other students, I enrolled in a Letters and Science curriculum. One should not be misled about the quality of the instruction at the University of Manitoba at that time. Almost the entire faculty had been trained at Oxford or Cambridge in England, but they were unable to find a position at a university in the United Kingdom because the job market there was very tight. These teachers therefore came to the Canadian prairies to await the call home to assume a proper post at one of the great English universities. In the meantime, they pretended they were at Oxbridge, and they set up exactly the same program of courses as they would have at the "real" university. They also had the very highest expectations of their students, just as they would have had back home. I didn't know that there were such places in the world! A place that assumed you were a good and serious person and where teachers expected excellent performance from everyone. I wasn't at St John's Technical High School any longer.

I was at "Oxford" in the prairies. For example, no attendance was ever recorded in any of my classes; we took one exam at the end of the year (not semester) and our grade was dependent on that one test. A variety of very detailed papers and essays were required on a weekly basis. I have never written as much or as fast as I did during my two years at the University of Manitoba. It was a daunting experience to write a detailed analysis (with a three-day deadline) of Hamlet's dilemma that would be read and critiqued by an Oxford don who had spent his entire adult life studying Shakespeare's play about the Prince of Denmark. We did all of Chaucer in a few weeks. And we read all of John Milton's *Paradise Lost* and *Paradise Regained* in a similar timeframe. Who could forget such Milton lines as "The mind is its own place, and in itself can make a heav'n of hell, a hell of heav'n"? Or Satan's thoughts as he begins to realize that he will be in hell for a very long time. He is still licking his wounds and is not yet seriously considering revenge. Instead, he is deciding how to make the best of the situation. It is a few lines later when he utters the famous phrase "Better to reign in hell, than serve in heav'n."

And we analyzed all of the Lake poets. We learned that the Lake Poets all lived in the Lake District of England at the turn of the nineteenth century. As a group, they followed no single "school" of thought or literary practice, but their poetry was seen as overly modern and experimental. *The Edinburgh Review* wrote a famously scathing review of the so-called Romantic Movement and of their scandalous work. The three main figures of what has become known as the Lake School were William Wordsworth, Samuel Taylor Coleridge, and Robert Southey. They were associated with several other poets and writers, including Dorothy Wordsworth, Charles Lloyd, Hartley Coleridge, John Wilson, and Thomas De Quincey. We knew all about this fascinating situation.

We studied not Canadian history but the history of England and of English royalty. The Battle of Hastings in 1066 is ingrained in my mind forever. As I am sure everyone knows, this battle (October 14, 1066) was the decisive victory in the Norman Conquest of England. It was fought between the Norman army of William the Conqueror, and the English army led by Harold Godwinson. The battle took place at Senlac Hill, approximately six miles northwest of Hastings.

The Norman army was estimated to number as many as 8,400 and consisted of 2,200 cavalry, 4,500 infantry, and 1,700 archers and crossbowmen. William's strategy relied on archers to soften the enemy, followed by a general advance of the infantry, and then a cavalry charge. His army was composed of nobles, mercenaries, and troops from France and Europe, including some from Southern Italy. The English army is usually thought to have numbered roughly 7,500 and consisted entirely of infantry. It is most probable that all the members of the army rode to battle, but once at the appointed place, they dismounted to fight on foot.

The battle was a decisive Norman victory. Harold II was killed; traditionally, it is believed he was shot through the eye with an arrow. Although there was further English resistance, this battle is seen as the point at which William gained control of England. The famous Bayeux Tapestry depicts the events before and during the battle. An abbey, known as Battle Abbey in East Sussex, was subsequently built on the site of the conflict.

Fascinating stuff. If you closed your eyes, you would swear you were in England. It was a remarkable, classical education. I really learned to write during those years. And I have never had my writing so brutally attacked as by these professors from England. But their criticism was nothing like that I suffered when putting in screws. The criticism I got for my writing was to help me be a better writer. It was not to prove my worthlessness. I began to realize that that there are two kinds of criticism. I probably learned more in those two years than I did in all the rest of my school years.

This lesson I learned about criticism is one that applies to my work even now. My students say that I am the toughest critic they have ever had. What they don't know is that I never criticize average students. I help average students gently, but

I would never really be critical. To me, that would be cruel. But if a student is outstanding, I want to help them be as good as they can be. My students all know that my intent is to be helpful, not destructive. I can't stand hearing someone criticize a person who has done his best and who is not likely to benefit from the assault. Kindness should be the goal. For both average students and for superstars.

14

IN THE LAND OF
MILK AND HONEY

Just as I was beginning to hit my academic stride, my father announced that the whole family was leaving Winnipeg. This happened in 1950 when I was eighteen years old. We were going to move to Los Angeles, California. The streets in California were paved with gold, and milk and honey flowed freely there. I have never understood whether my father's decision was a brave one or whether it was impetuous foolishness. I have heard from various sources over the years that the reason for this sudden decision was due to the fact that my father was in serious debt. There was no way he could extricate himself. Moving away was the best way to deal with this crisis.

My daughter asked me, "Why did you move to Los Angeles? Why didn't you stay in Winnipeg?" I was speechless. Stay in Winnipeg? It never occurred to me. It's true that I was having the time of my life at the university, but how could I turn down a chance to escape the North End? In spite of the wonderful chance I had to leave the battleground, it was not easy to leave my University of Manitoba. I often think of that place, fondly, as the Carnegie Library Plus.

My father made several serious errors in planning his escape from Winnipeg. One involved the purchase of a car for the trip. We could not afford a moving van, so my father decided to install a roof storage unit on our car and to haul a trailer. The problem was that our old car was not in good enough shape to survive this long trip and heavy load. He decided to buy a new car. Always scheming, he discovered that, before our trip, he and I could zip down to Minnesota, in the United States, and buy a new Chevrolet for a lot less money than it would cost in Canada. So the two of us made that trip to Minnesota and we did buy a new car a few miles south of the Canadian border (in a small town named Crookston), and we did save a lot of money. About a year later, living in California, my dad received a bill from the State of California requiring that he pay a "use tax." That tax was to compensate the State of California for the new car he brought into the state and on which he paid no sales tax. This unfortunate omission came to light when he registered his new car with the State Department of Motor Vehicles. The amount of that bill was more than we saved by buying the car in Minnesota.

The second error my dad made was in assuming that he could easily get a job once he arrived in the Promised Land. My dad had always been very proud of the fact that a skilled tradesman could always get a job anywhere in the world. That was one of his criticisms of me. He could not see how reading books was going to guarantee that I would always be able to find a job wherever I happened to be. In any case, we sold everything and moved many thousands of miles away to a place where my father had no job and no prospects for one, but where he knew everything would be OK. The first thing my father discovered upon arriving in Los Angeles was that he could not get a job as an electrician in that city without belonging to the union. And the long list of people waiting to join the union involved a wait of four years!

He was outraged. He asked the union official how he was expected to support his family while waiting four years for a union card. Then the union man made his mistake. He indicated in a very subtle way that there were ways to move up on the waiting list. And he intimated through various gestures that a monetary contribution would help enormously in prioritizing his application. The more money, the higher the priority. My father then knew he was not in the Prairies any longer. Welcome to the Big City. He refused to even consider this criminal deal.

So he found other menial work using his electrical knowledge, but he was not earning enough money to support the family. For that reason, my mother found a job and worked as a secretary. In her later years, she described this job as the first time in her life when she began to feel like a real person, a person of consequence. Her job was with one of the Hollywood studios, where a television show called *I Love Lucy* was being produced. She did typing and filing and telephone work and was paid well for her effort. She got dressed up and went to work every day and was treated like a contributing member of society. She also told me that, while she was working hard, it was better than being a princess.

Now my mother had stories to tell at the dinner table. She was involved in a small lunch group that would sit together and share experiences. That was a first for her. She went to a movie once with one of her coworkers. To a movie! In the evening. On her own. She did an excellent job in her work, and she was repeatedly promoted. She was being recognized as a person of intelligence and accomplishment. This, of course, was late in her life to finally be recognized as a real person (she was forty-five years old at the time), but as they say, "better late than never."

My father was eventually able to start his own electrical contracting business in Los Angeles. But it was a business with a major difference. His was the only electrical contracting company in Los Angeles that was nonunion. He remained so angry with the union official who wanted bribery money in order for him to get a union card that for the rest of his life he refused to have anything to do with the union. Every time he applied for a permit to do work in the city, the union was informed and they would set up a picket line to prevent his entrance or exit from the job. My father would then call the police and request an escort. Eventually, the union people lost interest in this renegade, but he remained antagonistic toward the union until he died.

My mother and father also began to have a social life in Los Angeles. My mother's brother, Chuck, was already living in Los Angeles with his actress wife, Frances. And many other Bay relatives were living there as well. I was still a dutiful son, and I would sometimes join the large group at "family gatherings." There were often more than fifty relatives in attendance at these events! People of whom I had never before heard. I had a hard time keeping track of all of them. All of them were relatives, mostly cousins. It turns out that when Eli and Gertrude and Max and Anne were assigned to the Canadian Prairies, other Jewish refugees from Russia and the Ukraine were assigned to new lands being developed in a place called California. In Los Angeles, Rose fit in easily (as a Bay) and Bob also did well—for two reasons: no one knew of his questionable background and, perhaps more importantly, he truly charmed them all. The California family was so big, with so many branches, that Rose and Bob slipped in almost without being noticed.

The Bay family in Los Angeles was dramatically different from the one in Winnipeg and Dauphin. The people in Los Angeles were glamorous and famous and wealthy and lived in places like Beverly Hills and Bel Air. My father felt that he was now in the sort of world to which he had always aspired. He wasn't rich, of course, but, in the end, he did manage to rent an apartment only a block away from the Beverly Hills town limit. When asked where he lived, he would say "Beverly Hills." It was almost true. And he was able to buy a Cadillac. It was an older model, but it *was* a Cadillac.

The extended Bay family in Los Angeles featured many wealthy and famous people who invited my parents to lunches and celebrations. It was a totally different world in which they found themselves. They met a young Michael Bay (who later became a famous movie director with such well-known movies as *Bad Boys, The Rock, Armageddon,* and *Transformers*). Michael Bay's cousin, Susan Bay, married the actor Leonard Nimoy. Frances Bay was beginning to receive accolades and fame for her roles in motion pictures and on the stage. She mainly played character roles as a quirky older woman (for example, the rye bread woman in a famous *Seinfeld* TV episode) or a feisty grandmother (for example, in the Adam Sandler movie *Happy Gilmore*). Her husband, Chuck Bay, was becoming a prosperous businessman who was importing very high quality goose feathers from Hungary and very high quality fabrics in order to manufacture super expensive down comforters. He was the man who introduced this product in the United States, and he made a lot of money doing so. If you were part of the Bay family, you could even get one of his comforters wholesale! So here my parents were, in the land of milk and honey, surrounded by famous people, and they were beginning to become part of it.

15

MY LIFE IN WESTWOOD VILLAGE

As Rose, Bob, and my sister Audrey settled into this new life and into their modest new home on Plymouth Boulevard (financed again with the help of Max Goffman, now a resident of Los Angeles), I went to the UCLA campus and applied for admission. My grades from the University of Manitoba were decent, and I was admitted as a junior. The officials in charge, however, said it was mandatory that I select a major. I didn't know what that was. And once I found out, I was not prepared to select a major at random. I was totally stumped. So here I was: I had been plucked from the North End of Winnipeg and Andrew Carnegie's library, and my family had few resources, and I was being confronted by a challenge that was totally beyond my abilities to deal. Great beginning in the land of milk and honey!

Fortunately, I was assigned an advisor who was very wise. Professor Philip Selznick. He was a famous and distinguished man who somehow sensed my dilemma and advised me to select a major called pre-legal. He pointed out that with this major, I could avoid my problem and take any courses I wanted. So I did that for the next two years.

There was one other complication affecting my new college career: I had no money. I suppose I could have asked my father for a loan, but (1) he did not have any money to spare and (2) I would not have asked him anyway. Whenever he gave me money, he always assumed that he had purchased stock in me and was therefore entitled to detailed reports about everything in my life. It was too high a price to pay. So I found five jobs. My first job was as an assistant to a paraplegic, Bob Wellman. I lived in an apartment with him, cooked and cleaned for him, and thereby earned my rent. My second job was in the university cafeteria, where I bussed dishes and washed the floors. For this I received free breakfasts and dinners. My third job was in the university bookstore, where I worked any free hours I had during the day and from which I actually earned real money. My fourth job was at Barker Brothers furniture store, where at 6:00 p.m., I showed up to vacuum rugs and pack boxes for shipping. More money. And finally, at midnight, I worked in a cleaning crew at Bullocks Department store in Westwood Village.

During that year, I bought a beat-up old (1939) Ford car. I needed it because the UCLA campus, located in Westwood Village, had a terrible public transit system, and I was basically isolated there without some form of personal transportation. The car cost me $100. I paid for it through a loan I negotiated with a relative. The loan came about because I was faced with a gigantic debt that was going to sink me. I had to pay my school registration fees ($45) plus buy an entire semester's books ($130). There was no way I could do that, even with my five jobs. I discovered the Student Aid Office on campus, and I applied for a loan. They were willing to loan me the money but only if I could get the signature of a cosigner—a responsible, solvent person who would guarantee payment if I defaulted. I visited the wealthiest family member I knew: my cousin

Max Bay, a wealthy accountant. He agreed to back me. He suggested, however, that I borrow $500 from the university so that I could pay for the books and fees and buy a car and have a little left over for emergencies.

The car decision turned out to be a big mistake. While it was good to have a way to leave Westwood now and then, the expense of having such a luxury was very high. For example, one day I was driving very slowly on Olympic Boulevard when I got into big trouble. I was driving slowly because I had no brakes. My brakes had given up their job about a week earlier. I had no brakes because I couldn't afford to fix them. This was not my cleverest moment. I naturally banged into a big new Buick while I was traveling five miles an hour on Olympic Boulevard. This was fast enough to cause a fairly big dent in my poor victim's fender. The man got out of his dented car and asked, "Can I see your insurance papers?" I said, "I don't have any insurance." He said, "How do you propose to deal with the damage you have caused?" I said, "I'm very sorry about this. I can't pay for the damage all at once. But if you tell me how much it costs to fix your car, I'll bring $5 to your house every week until the bill is paid." I didn't have a telephone number to give him, but I was at least able to provide him with my home address on campus. For some reason, the nice man believed me and trusted me, and we made a deal. I drove to his house in the Holmby Hills (close to Hugh Hefner's Playboy mansion and near UCLA) every single week after that until my debt was paid off. Later on the day of the accident, I also went to the Firestone store in Westwood Village and got my brakes fixed for an additional $1.25 per week. This was a low point.

I wasn't going to let my lack of money prevent me from doing other foolish things. At the end of my first year at UCLA, my friend Hal Kassarjian and I decided to travel to the East Coast to explore that part of America. Neither of us had any money to do that. We had heard, however, that people sometimes wanted a car moved from one coast to the other and were willing to hire a person to drive it for them. For them, this was apparently cheaper than shipping the car by train or truck. We searched the Want Ads in the *Los Angeles Times* and there it was! A woman wanted someone to drive her, and her brand-new Chrysler, to Philadelphia. Hal and I called her and made an appointment to meet and discuss this possibility. It turned out the lady was an elderly woman who did not know how to drive but she wanted to give the car to her brother as a birthday gift and she wanted to be there when he got it. She agreed to pay for the gas and for our hotel rooms and food, and we agreed to do the job. A free trip across the country!

We left two weeks later at the beginning of July. As we crossed the Sierra Mountains and entered Nevada, she said, "I have always wondered what Las Vegas was all about. Would you boys mind if we stopped there along the way so that I could have a peek? It won't take long." We agreed to do that. We traveled down the main street and looked at all the gambling casinos. (This was in 1951, and the era of the big hotels had not yet descended on Las Vegas.) Then she said, "Boys, would you mind parking here on the street so that I can pop in to one of these casinos? I'd like to see what they look like on the inside. I'll just be a few minutes." This was at 2:00 p.m. At 5:00 p.m., when she had not returned to the car, we went in to find her. There she was at the craps table with a big pile of chips in front of her. She said, "Oh, I'm so sorry I'm taking longer than I expected, but I just can't leave now! Here is some money. Go have dinner and we'll leave right after that."

We had dinner and, at 9:00 p.m., went in to find her again. She had an even bigger pile of chips now. She said, "Oh my! This is embarrassing! But I can't leave now! Would you mind taking a nap in the car? I'll be out real soon." At seven in the morning, we went back into the casino to find her, but this time, she had no chips in front of her. She was flat broke. She had spent all of our traveling money. She was in tears and was very apologetic about everything. She hoped we would forgive her and asked what were we going to do now. So there we were. Two totally inexperienced nineteen-year-old boys stranded in Las Vegas with a new car and a crying older woman.

Eventually, we decided to go on with the trip. Hal and I took turns driving so that one of us could nap. The reason for the constant napping was that we did not sleep at night. What we did every night was find a motel room for our former patron while we went to the local truck stop in town. There, we offered to help drivers unload their cargoes in town. We did that every night. And we made enough money doing this to pay for the motel room, gas, food and other expenses during the rest of the trip. We drove, napped, and worked our way to Philadelphia. We eventually delivered our "benefactor" and the car to her brother, and then Hal and I went our separate ways. He went on to Boston and I went to New York City.

In New York, I took a room at the cheapest hotel in town, the YMCA. It was a tiny, tiny room with a cot and a dresser. I began my sightseeing only to discover that the heat and humidity during the day was more than I could deal with. I solved that problem by getting a job as an usher in an air-conditioned movie theater during the day and reserved my sightseeing for the evenings. That was back in the days when movie theaters still had ushers. We had a little uniform and a flashlight, and we helped people find their way to seats. For two weeks, I saw the same movie over and over. Alec Guinness in the *Lavender Hill Mob*. I knew the script by heart. Fortunately, it was a very good movie.

In the evenings, I traveled everywhere—Manhattan, the Bronx, Brooklyn and Coney Island, Queens, Staten Island. I went to the Library (of course), to the Empire State Building, Radio City Music Hall, Rockefeller Center, Forty-second Street, the Statue of Liberty, and more. It was a wonderful two weeks. And throughout, I was very careful about my money. I thought I had saved enough for my bus trip back to Los Angeles, but when I finally went to the bus station to arrange for my journey home, I was stunned when I saw how much money the Greyhound people actually wanted! I certainly hadn't been able to save that much! I wandered away in a daze until I saw a sign erected by a new bus company advertising a much cheaper ticket. I went to the Trailways Terminal and saw this big gleaming bus sitting there. Easily as nice as the Greyhound bus. It had a toilet and air-conditioning, and the ticket was much less than Greyhound. I bought a ticket and had money left over.

With that settled, I went to Macy's basement store and bought a cheap cardboard suitcase. On my way to the terminal the next morning, my new suitcase burst open in the middle of Times Square. I had to buy some twine to hold it together. It was not a pretty sight. I boarded my bargain-priced but fancy, gleaming bus, and we left New York headed for California. All went well for thirty minutes. In New Jersey, our beautiful bus broke down, and we all had to board a substitute bus that miraculously appeared soon after we were forced to stop. Unfortunately, the substitute vehicle was a beat-up old bus with no toilet and no air-conditioning. As we left in the substitute bus, I happened to look back at the beautiful broken down bus and, to my amazement, saw that it had turned back and was headed to Manhattan. To pick up more suckers, I presume. All in all, my trip to the East Coast that summer was very educational. On many levels.

As I began my second year at UCLA, I realized that I could no longer continue looking after Bob Wellman. I was exhausted with the work required to keep him going, and I therefore took a very inexpensive apartment near the university. It was cheap because it didn't have a kitchen. But I was eating at the school cafeteria for free anyway so that worked out for me. With these jobs, I was able to live a reasonable life and continue my studies. I still had no idea at all where I was heading in this work. I just did my homework and other assignments in a more or less mindless way. I was by now well-trained in this kind of routine, and I was simply still trying not to be useless.

While my life was more or less manageable, my poverty was a definite issue. For example, the university cafeteria was closed on the weekend and my meal source was therefore gone. Normal kids in my circumstance might have gone home for food, but I chose not to do this. Other kids might have been invited to a party now and then where free food would have been available, but I had few friends. I was working or studying every hour of every day, and this left little time for making friends. I basically went without food on the weekend (except for the small amounts of food I had stolen from the cafeteria during the week; I assume the statute of limitations applies and that I cannot now be arrested for this crime.) Perhaps this explains why, at a height of six feet, I weighed only 130 pounds.

Then one day in 1953, in my last semester as a senior, Professor Ruth Reimer asked me if I would like to become a graduate student and be a teaching assistant. She explained that the University would pay me to continue my studies. I jumped at the chance. Professor Reimer was a professor of sociology and the teaching assistant job was in the Department of Sociology, and that is the only explanation I have for how I came to major in sociology. I followed the money. I am not very proud of this and I wish I had a more elegant and thoughtful explanation for this life-changing decision, but I do not.

Life became a little easier then. I also received a Will Roger's Scholarship that provided some money and that helped too. It was during this time that I began dating Marilyn Egenes, a girl I had met while working in the bookshop. We were married the next year, in 1954. I was twenty-two years old. She was twenty-three. I was attracted to Marilyn because she thought I was wonderful. She may have been the first person since my Winnipeg days who thought I was a prince. She had another attractive feature: she was not Jewish. At some level in my mind, I think I resolved to avoid duplicating the Jewish scene that I had experienced in Dauphin and Winnipeg, so the fact that Marilyn was not Jewish was very appealing to me. Marilyn's family was Lutheran. Her mother and father were shocked when they discovered my background. And my parents were shocked when they learned of Marilyn's background. Many hours were spent in dealing with both sets of parents. Both Marilyn and I asked for our parents' understanding (and approval) but neither of us was going to change our mind if they decided not to support us. In the end, both my parents and Marilyn's parents gave their half-hearted and hesitant blessings. Marilyn and I were married in a small ceremony in a nondenominational ceremony in Alhambra, California, a location midway between my parent's home in Los Angeles and Marilyn's parent's home in San Gabriel.

I was attracted to Marilyn because she thought I could do no wrong. I think Marilyn was interested in me because I was a serious student who had no time for frivolity. She would say, "Let's go to a movie," and I would say, "Sorry. I have too much work to do." She hadn't met such a boy in her life. For reasons that are still beyond me, she found that attractive. Apparently, not many young men are furiously working to accomplish something about which they had no understanding. And apparently not many young men desperately need to be seen as royalty. Marilyn herself was an extraordinarily hardworking young woman from a modest working class background. We found much in common.

Marilyn's father, Byron Egenes, ran away from his Iowa home when he was still in high school and he made his way (where else?) to the land of milk and honey in Los Angeles. He got a job delivering bread to doorsteps and later got a job with the Western Union Company. He delivered telegrams and eventually became the manager of a little Western Union shop. It was there that he met his future wife, Elaine. Byron later became a carbon paper salesman. He and Elaine lived in a modest neighborhood, Southgate, where they raised Marilyn and her younger brother, Lloyd. Marilyn was a very talented singer early in her life, and she was determined to enroll in the Music Department at UCLA but her family could not afford to help her go to the university. She therefore dropped out of school and took a clerical job at the Aluminum Corporation of America where she worked for one year, saving all her money so that she could make it to UCLA. When I met her, she was still supporting herself by working at the UCLA bookstore, even while she was attending classes full time. She was in a demanding music program along with the actress Carol Burnett and the musician Lotfi Mansouri (who later became director of the San Francisco Opera Company), but she was able to do both jobs because she worked as hard on her mission as I did on mine.

By the time I entered graduate school, Marilyn had graduated as an opera major from UCLA and she had gone on to work as a secretary in the Music Department. She had a once-in-a-generation mezzo soprano voice and she had won every singing contest in which she had ever participated. When I proposed marriage to her, she was ready to apply for a Fulbright scholarship to study music in Italy, and I interrupted those plans. Instead, she worked as a secretary while I studied for my master's degree, but she also sang in several local concert halls during that year. To great acclaim.

I received my master's degree in 1955. I had been told during my last year of studies at UCLA that a master's degree in sociology would not be very a useful in finding a job—my advisors thought that I really needed a Ph.D. degree. So during that year, I applied to seven Ph.D. programs around the country. I was accepted by all seven, but I chose the one that offered the most fellowship money. The following year, I entered the Medical Sociology program (the very first ever offered in the world) at Yale University. Once again, this was probably not the most thoughtful way to make such an important decision about my life.

I have given some thought to the question of how we make important decisions when those decisions have major consequences for our lives. I suppose the proper way to make such decisions is to compose a list of the advantages and disadvantages associated with various options and carefully weigh and compare them. In my life, I think I have more often taken advantage of opportunities as they appeared and I'm not sure how thoughtful I have been about the pros and cons. I can't believe, however, that I have been totally mindless. For example, while it might look as if I casually took advantage of the first opportunity that presented itself, I think that, at some subconscious level, I must also have rejected many other unsuitable opportunities. Malcolm Gladwell has referred to this kind of decision making as "thin slicing." In his book, *Blink*, Gladwell refers to our ability to gauge what is really important from a very narrow period of experience. He suggests that spontaneous decisions are often as good as—or even better than—carefully planned and considered ones. Or as Yogi Berra once said, "When you come to a fork in the road, take it!"

16

FROM DAUPHIN TO
THE IVY LEAGUE

Marilyn and I flew across the country on a propeller driven Trans World Airways Constellation airplane in the summer of 1955 to begin our new life in New Haven, Connecticut. We were both flying in an airplane for the first time in our lives. Cousins in Los Angeles, the Finklesteins, gave us new Samsonite suitcases for our trip. Neither of us had ever owned our own real suitcases. The whole experience was a major life event.

So we arrived at Yale University like two country bumpkins with eyes wide open and astonished by everything. Aside from my brief two-week adventure in New York City, neither of us had ever really been to the East Coast, let alone to a university anything like Yale. I will never forget the invitation we received from the Yale faculty to attend a Welcoming Tea. I had never heard of a "welcoming tea." We entered the elegant wood-paneled room and passed through a reception line. This was the first time I had ever heard the word "reception line." We lined up to get our cups of tea poured by the wife of the

Chairman of the Department, Mrs. Hollingshead (not to be confused with the New Jersey Hollingshead who invented the drive-in movie theater!) She was standing at a large silver Samovar-type tea dispenser, wearing little white gloves, and we each received our tea in delicate English bone china teacups. I had never seen such a ceremony in my life. As you can perhaps sense, there were a lot of firsts occurring during a compressed time period. Fortunately, as an upwardly mobile survivor, I had become quite skilled in picking up important clues regarding dress, attitude, manners, and behavior, but the Yale episode pushed me to the limits of my ability.

Shortly after arriving at Yale, I met another survivor, Sim Warkov. Sim was a doctoral student in the Department of Sociology. I met him when he gave a great seminar on his thesis topic: Why do tuberculosis patients leave TB sanitaria against medical advice? The traditional way of studying this problem was to study the characteristics of people who left compared to those who did not leave. Sim instead compared the "leaving" rate among the sanitaria. How did the institutions with high "leaving" rates differ from those with low rates? Fascinating. When I talked to him after his session, I was astonished to learn that he too came from the North End of Winnipeg! He even had attended my great-grandfather's Hebrew School, the Talmud Torah! But Sim was a few years older than I was and he lived a long six blocks from my street, so our paths did not cross in those days. During Sim's working life, he was a professor of sociology at the University of Connecticut but, now retired, he lives in Corte Madera, California, a few miles west of where I live! He has taken on a new life since then, learning modern dance and writing poetry. We see each other occasionally and, at our last meeting, he gave me a copy of his new book of poetry, *Thin Soils*, based on his early days in Winnipeg. He knows my stories and I know his. That we both felt the need to describe our early days in the frozen North is, to me, remarkable.

While I got ready to begin my doctoral studies, Marilyn got a job at Blue Cross of Connecticut as the manager of a stenography pool. In those days, doctors filed their reports to Blue Cross on recording tape, and twenty women were employed transcribing those tapes onto paper. Marilyn sat at the front of this room and supervised these women. She helped them to spell tough medical words, settled interpersonal problems, arranged their vacation schedules, and so on. Not the most fascinating or challenging job in the world, but it paid well. She also traveled to New York on many weekends to sing in various musical groups there. That all stopped one day.

On one of those weekends, Marilyn went to New York to audition for a very prestigious and competitive position in a singing group (Musica Antiqua) that would record selections of ancient music. Over one hundred women were at that audition. While Marilyn was a truly outstanding singer who had previously won important prizes at every concert in which she had performed, almost all of the one hundred contestants at this audition were as good as she was! This had never happened to her before. The audition people made it clear to all of them that sheer singing talent was no longer the deciding issue. They were all talented. The issue was whether they were ready to devote themselves twenty-four hours a day, seven days a week, to this mission. For the first time, Marilyn had to decide how badly she wanted a full-time musical career. Was she willing to devote her life to singing? She had never been pushed this hard before. In the end, she decided not to do it. She wanted a family and she could not see herself resigning from "normal life" to pursue a very focused career in singing. This was an emotional weekend for her.

Marilyn's decision not to devote her life to singing had an unfortunate and unanticipated consequence. She could not find other venues that would allow her to keep singing at her distinguished level. When she joined community choirs and other similar groups, the skill of the singers and the conductor was so much lower than what she had been accustomed to, she ended up being very frustrated. She eventually found a church that welcomed her as a soloist and later, a synagogue, where she learned and sang Hebrew songs! That synagogue was a famous one: the rabbi there (Robert Goldburg) provided instruction in the Jewish faith to Marilyn Monroe after she married the playwright Arthur Miller. As a consequence of this notoriety, the synagogue was full every weekend, and Marilyn became a local "star." These singing opportunities were moderately satisfying. I learned then that there is no "middle ground" for supremely talented people. Either you devote your life to your talent or you must find an entirely different way to be happy.

While these events were unfolding, I went daily to the Yale campus to begin life as a doctoral student in medical sociology. The Commonwealth Fund of New York had provided Yale with money to support this new Ph.D. program. There were four of us in the first cohort. As I mentioned earlier, this was the first program in medical sociology ever offered anywhere, and none of us was sure in what direction things should go. The four of us were given a choice early on as to whether we would focus on what was then called the sociology of medicine or sociology in medicine. The sociology of medicine option dealt with things like the institution of medicine and medical care, the sick role, and the attitudes and beliefs of patients regarding illness, pain, and medical treatment. There was already quite a bit of literature and research on these issues, and if we chose that route, we would have a fairly easy time in connecting the dots. Three of my group made a wise decision and chose to go in that direction. In contrast, I decided to pursue the sociology in medicine option. In my understanding, that choice was concerned with understanding how the way we live affects our health and well-being. That seemed to me to be a much more important and interesting challenge. Unfortunately, very little had ever been done to study these issues, and I was basically on my own.

It is difficult to now look back and understand my choice. It was a pivotal decision, and it changed forever the trajectory of my life. I wish I could tell a rational and reasonable story to justify my thinking. I cannot. The best I can do is say that I felt I needed to stand out to survive. I didn't want to follow the crowd. I needed to hang a shingle that proclaimed my independence and uniqueness. I needed to do it my way. I had already been deeply affected by the way life in the North End influenced the life chances of people who lived there. Those pressures affected their choices, thoughts, aspirations, hopes, and, perhaps, their health. It seemed important to me that it would be good if we better understood those social pressures. Especially if those pressures were unfair.

I learned later that the risky choice I made was endorsed and approved by my professor, August B. Hollingshead, because he had his own hidden agenda. At that time, he and a professor of psychiatry in the Yale Medical School, Dr. Fritz Redlich, were just beginning a groundbreaking, very large, and complicated study of how the social class position of people influenced their mental health. They regarded their now classic work as belonging to the field of sociology in medicine. So they saw me as a person who would help them with their work. If I would be willing to do my doctoral thesis on their project, they thought that they would be able to get free help on their project and I would be able to complete a doctoral thesis. It was, in their view, a win-win situation.

I probably should have followed their advice and done my thesis on the topic of mental health. But I did not. I felt that if I worked with them, I would end up being an assistant to these great and famous people and that I would not be able to make my own special contribution. I was a prince wasn't I? And I needed to do something really special to prove my dad wrong, didn't I? I had been doing things alone and in my own way for many years now, so I suppose this choice was not that unusual. I chose a thesis topic that no one in the world had ever worked on. Foolhardy? Probably. Naive? Certainly.

I chose to work on the problem of infertility. I had been reading some papers showing that one-third of all infertile couples got pregnant within three months of coming to an infertility clinic *regardless of their diagnosis or the treatment they received at the clinic.* That made no sense and was a much talked-about mystery. I connected with Dr. Luigi Mastroianni, a young gynecologist in the Infertility Clinic of the Yale School of Medicine, and he helped me to design a project to see if I could shed any light on this interesting question.

My findings were provocative but raised more questions than they answered. I checked the clinic records and made a note of all the patients who had called the clinic to make an appointment but who never showed up at the clinic. Then I went to the homes of these people to interview them. Quite a few of them had already become pregnant even though they had not received any medical care. I also made a list of all the patients who had completed one appointment at the clinic and who then quit coming. I went to their homes and interviewed them as well. Quite a few of them had also gotten pregnant even though they had done nothing after their first clinic visit.

I also interviewed patients who had completed their treatment program and who had been told their case was hopeless. Quite a few of them also became pregnant after they received this news. Same story for those who were discharged with the diagnosis that they seemed fine and they should just keep trying. Same story for those who decided to give up and adopt a baby. Same story for those who actually filed papers to adopt. And same story for those who actually did adopt a baby. In the end, I had accounted for about 85 percent of the spontaneous conceptions among this group of patients. I concluded my thesis by suggesting that the common denominator in each of these groups of patients was that they had given up trying. They each gave up for different reasons, but they all gave up. I suggested that future research should focus on the physiologic consequences associated with "giving up."

This research project was my first effort to explore the idea that the way in which we think has important consequences for our health. All of the work that had previously been done on infertility had focused on endocrine hormones and anatomy. While these factors were clearly important, there obviously was more going on. For the next fifty years, my research has continued to explore these early ideas in more depth. How do social and psychological forces "get into the body" to affect our health? My thesis was a good beginning, and it strengthened my determination to do things "my way."

17

PREPARING TO ENTER
THE WORKFORCE

When I finished my thesis and graduated from Yale
in 1957, I was twenty-five years old and was now slated to
become an officer in the army to fight in Korea. Professor
Hollingshead said that I might want to consider an alternative
that would give me a military deferment: go to work for the
U.S. Public Health Service in Washington. I agreed to do that,
and in fact, I spent the next ten years of my life in the Public
Health Service as a government worker. Those ten years of
my life, from 1958 to 1968, were tortuous and difficult for me.
I had entered the government workforce but I found it very
challenging to fit in. The government is not the best place to
be if you are trying to hang a shingle. The government does
not honor "doing it your way." But now I was a married man,
and during those ten years, we had three children. I needed to
earn a steady income, and I was trying to be good boy. I hung
in. Not easily, or happily, but I did hang in.

The first of my government jobs was in Washington DC
and I resigned from it after two years. My next job was at the

National Institutes of Health in Bethesda, Maryland, and I resigned from that job after two years as well. I then worked in the Public Health Service Hospital in San Francisco, California for six years, and then, you got it, I resigned yet again. It should be said that I did these jobs quite well. Despite being hard, those ten years were not wasted years. In fact, when I resigned from the government, I had done well enough to be appointed as a full professor at the University of California at Berkeley. There are two unusual things about that. First, aside from a few very senior and distinguished scholars, people tend not to be immediately appointed to full professor positions at major universities. They are typically appointed at lower levels and then work their way up to that senior level. Second, I was only thirty-six years of age at the time.

Why was I struggling in these jobs? As you might be able to tell from the Ph.D. episode at Yale, I did not fit into the usual molds very easily. All the people in my Yale class did conventional Ph.D. dissertations, and I chose to do something no one else had done before. My three jobs in the government all required me to do things that were not what I had in mind for myself. I was not able "to do my thing," but rather, I had to do what other people had in mind for me. This was a challenge for me. I may already have mentioned, once or twice, that I was a Prince after all! I needed a job where I was not dependent on others to survive. Bureaucracies are not designed to deal with people like me. When I finally was appointed to a tenured position at a first-rate university, I had found my place. I have (happily) remained in that job now for forty-three years. So far. Not bad.

18

WORK IN WASHINGTON

As I mentioned before, my first job was in Washington. Professor Hollingshead said that he had found me a good job in the U.S. Public Health Service that would exempt me from serving in the army and fighting in Korea. He said that he had recently talked to a statistician in the Heart Disease Control Program in Washington who wanted to hire a sociologist. So I took the train to Washington, got a tiny room in the Harrington Hotel (Washington's "oldest continuously operating hotel") and, the next morning, went to meet Phillip Enterline. I asked him why he wanted to hire a sociologist to study heart disease, and he said that he was not sure. He and his group had just completed a study of the geographic distribution of coronary heart disease mortality in the U.S., and they found very high rates on the East and West Coasts of the country and in the Detroit-Chicago metropolitan area, but low rates elsewhere. After two years of research on this, they had not been able to explain this finding, and they thought perhaps a sociologist might be able to help.

So I took the job. Marilyn and I borrowed a car from a friend, and we hauled all of our stuff to Washington where we found a little apartment. By this time, Marilyn was pregnant with our first child, Karen. We drove the loaded car to Washington and found an apartment in Alexandria, Virginia. We stayed in that apartment for only a few months. Marilyn had come to realize that if we were ever going to be able to buy a house, we needed to begin saving money immediately. I, of course, paid no attention to this. On her own, Marilyn figured out a way to solve our problem. While I was working in Washington, she arranged for us to live at the Groveton Motel on Highway 1 in Alexandria, Virginia. The deal she worked out was this: we would occupy a small four-room house on the motel grounds at half price and, in exchange, we would look after the other ten motel units for a retired Southern gentleman, Colonel (ret) Carlisle Burdette. Those motel units were occupied for three to six months at a time by young married army couples. The young men were in training at Fort Belvoir near Alexandria. Their wives worked at jobs in the town of Alexandria. Marilyn's job was to rent the motel units when they became available. My never-ending job was to mow the enormous two-acre lawn every week.

While I was a student at Yale, I really began to develop my own style of working and thinking. I took the road less often traveled, and I was now getting ready to continue my adventure in my new job in Washington. I was not alone in learning to be my own person. Marilyn was my partner in the adventure. The Groveton Motel was one minor manifestation of her creativity and cleverness. There was more to her than that. She actually had an impact on how we, as Americans, deal with childbearing. I mentioned earlier that when we moved to Washington, Marilyn was pregnant with our first child. While we were still in New Haven, Marilyn was seeing an obstetrician at Yale to help her with the pregnancy. In her fourth month of pregnancy, Dr. Grantly Dick-Reid visited Yale from England to discuss his radical new approach to childbirth.

Dr. Dick-Reid is regarded as the father of the natural childbirth movement. He dedicated his life to educating expectant parents about the benefits of giving birth naturally, with as little intervention as possible from obstetricians and health professionals. Much of the pain in childbirth, he argued, came from society's attitude toward childbirth, which often emphasized the pain. Dick-Read's ideas were at first ridiculed, and he was expelled from the London clinic he had set up with a group of fellow obstetricians. The publication of his first book, *Natural Childbirth*, was greeted with much opposition among his medical colleagues in London. It was only much later, when he published *Childbirth Without Fear*, that his philosophy captured the public's imagination. In his visit to Yale, he brought to America these ideas for the first time. The entire medical faculty at Yale bought into his thinking, and Marilyn became an enthusiastic member of this radical movement.

When I took the job in Washington, Marilyn had a dilemma. She talked to her doctor about who in Washington would help her with her natural childbirth approach to pregnancy. Her Yale doctor was not optimistic. Outside of New Haven, virtually no one had heard of this crazy idea. He said, "Marilyn, I don't know of anyone in Washington who gets it. I'll refer you to my friend at the George Washington Medical School. He is chairman of their Department of Obstetrics and Gynecology, and he may be your best bet." When we got to Washington, Marilyn visited him and told him her story. He was horrified! He said, "Marilyn, I have no idea what you are talking about, and I will not support you in this approach. I'll be your doctor but you are on your own with this natural childbirth idea."

So Marilyn reached out and invited a group of four pregnant women to work together and help each other in their pioneering pregnancies. They met once a week using *Childbirth Without Fear* as their Bible. From time to time, they invited a selected doctor to talk to them about a specific issue and, after the presentation, the doctor would then be asked to leave the meeting. When she appeared at the George Washington Hospital on January 23, 1958, to deliver our baby, I was there with her, stopwatch and notes in hand, doing all the things I had been trained to do as a "partner." As her time for delivery approached, dozens of medical students, interns, residents, and physicians began to gather near the delivery room to observe this woman engage in her nontraditional, weird behavior. She happily delivered our daughter without any anesthesia, and she wowed all the observers! One and a half years later, she appeared at the same place to deliver our son, David, and this time, it was no longer such an unusual phenomenon. In the short interval between these two births, natural childbirth was already becoming standard medical practice. By the time our third child (Janet) was born four years later, this method of childbirth was hardly worthy of note. Medical people no longer even blinked an eye.

I was beginning a new field of health research, and Marilyn was helping to usher in a new style of obstetrics. We were quite a couple. Marilyn also spurred interest in another uncommon activity for the times: she decided to breastfeed her daughter! Breastfeeding had virtually disappeared in America, except among poor, rural people. The prevalence of breastfeeding at that time was about 20 percent. I remember the time when we bought a book by Dr. Niles Newton called *Maternal Emotions* that explained how to successfully breastfeed a baby. (There is still one copy of this book available at Amazon for only $124!) Marilyn recruited another small group of women to read this book and to support one another in breastfeeding. These women were up against some formidable opposition: pediatricians were willing to support breastfeeding as long as babies got enough milk. If mothers were having any difficulties in producing sufficient milk, pediatric advice was to "supplement" breastfeeding with formula. This, as we now know, is the best way to sabotage a breastfeeding program. The support of other mothers in "hanging in" to a breastfeeding regimen is essential if the program is going to be successful.

All of this was taking place in 1958. I always thought that Marilyn's work preceded the formation of La Leche league, but I later learned that La Leche was established in Chicago in 1956. None of us in Washington were aware of that. We thought we were on the cutting edge.

While Marilyn was involved in changing the childbirth world, I went to work at the Heart Disease Program. Unfortunately, I learned on my first day of work that I was to be classified as a "Statistician." This was because there was no category available for a "Sociologist" in the Civil Service personnel system. This did not make much difference to me, but when I reported this to Professor Hollingshead, he went into orbit. Here was his student on the brink of making history in Washington, and instead, that student was going to be treated as a normal person. "A statistician indeed! If there's no category for a sociologist in the Civil Service, make one!" he snapped. He raised such a fuss that the government people did in fact establish that category. So I was the first sociologist labeled as such in the United States Civil Service.

Then I began my work. It was not a very happy story. I decided to do research on data from a state with a very low death rate from coronary heart disease with the idea of then doing a similar study in a higher rate state. We obtained some wonderful data from North Dakota, a low rate State.

In a six-county area of North Dakota, we were able to obtain information on every case of coronary heart disease that occurred in men, thirty-five to sixty-four years of age, in a one-year period. Then we selected two age-matched men, free of coronary heart disease, from a representative sample of the six county area from which the cases came. I then set about testing all the hypotheses that I had learned in graduate school. In those days, we were thinking about concepts such as marginality, status crystallization, and many other ideas that few scholars can now remember. It must be recognized, of course, that I had no literature or previous research to rely on. This was, I think, the first such study of coronary heart disease ever done by looking at social factors. So I based my work on the concepts that I had been studying in school. I spent a year doing this. Not one of the hypotheses worked out. The cases and controls did not differ from one another on any of the dozens and dozens of ideas that were then popular in sociology. I think Phil Enterline must have thought he made a major mistake in hiring me.

So I decided on a different tack. I decided to abandon all the theories I had been taught in school, and instead, I decided I would examine all of the data and see on which items there were similarities and difference between cases and controls. I had been taught that this type of fishing expedition was not a very good way to proceed, but I was desperate. In this analysis, I was able to see a considerably higher rate of coronary heart disease among men who had changed jobs and who had moved geographically and, especially, among men who had moved from farms to white-collar jobs in the city. I observed all of this, of course, after controlling for smoking, blood pressure, and many other coronary heart disease risk factors. I called this phenomenon "cultural mobility." Those men who had moved from one "world" to another had the highest rates of disease.

I was then able to repeat this analysis with a remarkably similar data set in a state with a much higher rate of coronary heart disease, California. And I found precisely the same thing as in North Dakota.

I came to a fateful decision based on this experience. I decided that the theories being talked about in sociology were not very useful in helping us think about health matters. I decided to stop basing my research on these theories. I argued, instead, that we should collect good data, do fishing expeditions, and develop new ideas about what was going on. I was set on developing a new field instead of relying on work that had been done by others. I, in fact, taught several generations of students to forget the "theory thing" and just go for it. The result is that we now in social epidemiology have piles and piles of findings and no way to make sense of it all or to think about what needs to be done next. My strategy had led my field down a blind alley. This sorry situation is not all my fault, of course, but I have been a major contributor. And the reason for it is to be found in the wheat fields of North Dakota. Fortunately, better minds than mine now prevail and things are getting better. For example, one of my former students, Nancy Krieger, now a professor at Harvard, is forcefully demonstrating the power, and importance, of theory in spite of everything I tried to teach her. I mention this only to point out that I have made my share of mistakes and bad decisions. But I try to learn from them.

While I was struggling with these data from North Dakota, I was prevailed upon by a very famous epidemiologist, Professor Jeremiah Stamler of Northwestern University in Chicago, to present my findings at a meeting of the American Heart Association that was being held in Miami, Florida. It was a daunting experience. Here was the useless kid from Dauphin making a speech before some of the most eminent cardiovascular authorities in the nation. They were all lined up in the first few rows wondering what this young skinny kid might have to say. Among them was Dr. Paul Dudley White, who had just treated President Dwight Eisenhower after his heart attack. I suggested to this audience that above and beyond the usual coronary heart disease risk factors was a set of social factors that no one had heard about before. My findings were controversial, and many people in the audience suggested to me later that I stop this work and return to research on more conventional topics. They said, "Stick with the things we already know about. Stick with the really important risk factors—high serum cholesterol levels, cigarette smoking, high blood pressure. Why get involved with studies of unknown factors such as the social determinants of disease?"

I did not stop, of course, but these were difficult times. I had other troubles on other fronts too. For example, a nutritionist on the staff of the Heart Disease Control Program, Marjorie Cantoni, asked me to help her design a dietary questionnaire. These were the days before we had the well-established instruments we have today. She wanted to do a study of Seventh-day Adventists. At that time in the late 1950s, there was a growing body of evidence, and speculation, that a diet high in fat might be a risk factor for coronary heart disease. Seventh-day Adventists were lacto-ovo-vegetarians, and Marjorie thought it would be interesting to study their serum cholesterol levels to see if their low-fat diets resulted in low levels of cholesterol. I agreed to help her design a questionnaire. As we worked, it occurred to me that Adventists might have lower cholesterol levels not only because of their diet but because they were religious. So I convinced her to let me add three questions at the end of the interview about their church attendance and about the importance of religion in their lives. Since this was a government survey, all forms for such research had to be cleared by the U. S. Bureau of the Budget. Two weeks after we submitted our questionnaire, word came that the questionnaire had been approved but that my three questions on religion had been deleted. I was not very happy. Upon inquiry, I was informed that there is in the U.S. Constitution this little policy about the separation of church and state and that my three questions, on a government form, violated the Constitution.

I handed in my resignation the next morning. How could they do this to me? I had tried to do my own thing, and now I was being thwarted by some rule regarding church and state? I often make fun of myself by saying that I am an arrogant, elitist, prima donna, and this rejection of my plan may have brought this character trait to the fore.

An Assistant Surgeon General summoned me to his office later that afternoon. "What's all this about quitting?" he asked. I told him that as a sociologist I needed to ask people questions about their lives, including their religious beliefs, and if I wasn't going to be able to do that, there was no point in my working in the government. He told me to calm down. He asked if there was any evidence to support my hypothesis that religious beliefs had anything to do with serum cholesterol levels.

"Of course there is!" I lied. "That's why I put those questions in!"

"OK," he said, "bring me the evidence and then we'll talk."

I went to poor suffering Phil Enterline and asked him for three weeks off so that I could search for the evidence that I had so confidently said existed.

I worked very hard during those three weeks, and I did in fact find quite a bit of evidence. There was information about religion and stress taken from studies of Trappist and Benedictine monks, and there was evidence about stress and cholesterol levels from studies of medical students at exam time and from tax accountants at tax time. I also did a lot of research about the Seventh-day Adventist religion and its relevance for stress research. As a complete amateur, I concluded that the Seventh-day Adventist religion was based on the return of the Lord and that his return will occur soon after we see people warring with one another and when there is much civil strife. So I argued, Seventh-day Adventists have a very different response than the rest of us when they read in the daily newspaper that everything is falling apart. We moan about the events of the day while they see the bad news as bringing them closer to salvation. I wrote a forty-five-page paper about stress and cholesterol levels, about religion and stress, and about the Seventh-day Adventist religion. It was, I must say, quite elegant. I ended with a paragraph saying that in light of the foregoing, the three questions I wanted to ask were clearly warranted.

I handed in my paper and was summoned a few days later to the assistant surgeon general's office. He said he was impressed with my paper and that he was satisfied that there was a credible scientific basis for my three questions. "But," he said, "we now have to consider the constitutional issue." I felt betrayed and said I was going to resign. Again, he told me calm down. "Give me a few weeks," he said. Several months later, a change in government policy about such issues was announced. One can now ask about things like religion if a case can be made that more good than harm will come from the inquiry. There has to be a good, or even compelling, reason for violating the constitution, but it can be done.

By then, I was being asked to be a consultant to the staff of the State Health Departments in Region V of the country (Michigan, Illinois, Indiana, Ohio, Minnesota, and Wisconsin). I would visit the Rheumatic Heart Disease staff in Illinois and advise them on their work! It was ridiculous. Here I was, a twenty-seven-year-old neophyte, advising much more senior people about things I knew little about. In the end, I couldn't take it anymore, and I resigned again. My assistant surgeon general friend interviewed me again to find out what was bothering me this time. I told him I needed a research job where I could learn more about actually doing research. I was too young to be an advisor. I needed a post-doctoral research position. He said he had just the job for me. Go to the National Institutes of Health, he said, and become an executive secretary in one of their study sections. I would then be able to work with the best researchers in the country and have enough time left over to do my own research as well. He said it would be perfect for me. "I'll make a few phone calls," he said.

19

ON TO THE NATIONAL INSTITUTES OF HEALTH

A year later, in 1960, I was invited to take a new job at the National Institutes of Health in Bethesda, Maryland. Marilyn and I with our two children, Karen and David, moved to Bethesda in July of that year. Karen was two and a half years old, and David was six months old. We bought our very first house in Bethesda using the money that Marilyn had accumulated in her work at the Groveton Motel. It was a small house about two miles away from the National Institutes of Health. The house cost $18,000 and required a down payment of $900. That would have ordinarily been much more money than we could have afforded, but we were able to do it with savings from the Groveton Motel adventure. I say "we" did it, but Marilyn is the one who made that happen because of her creativity and foresight.

My job at the National Institutes of Health was to establish, for the first time, an epidemiology study section. Study sections at the National Institutes of Health consist of national authorities who are invited to serve as reviewers of research grant applications and to decide which of them get funded and which get rejected. Being the executive secretary for one of these groups was a very powerful position for a twenty-eight-year-old beginner. The task of this new study section was to review the research grant applications that were being submitted to the National Institutes of Health dealing with the epidemiology of such noninfectious diseases as arthritis, mental illness, cancer, heart disease, and injuries.

This was to be the first time that work on the epidemiology of noninfectious diseases was formally recognized anywhere in the world. I had received my Ph.D. in the new field called medical sociology just three years prior to starting this job, and while I had been working as a fledgling epidemiologist in the heart disease program in the U.S. Public Health Service, I was not very knowledgeable about this brand-new discipline. Of course, not many other people were either. In fact, soon after I accepted the job, I was informed that we could not use the word "epidemiology" in the title of the new study section because that word was only to be used in regard to the well-established field of infectious diseases. We reluctantly came up with another name (Human Ecology). Five years later, common sense prevailed, and an epidemiology study section was created that dealt with both infectious and noninfectious diseases. In time, that study section grew so large that it was subdivided into several groups.

As I began to work to set up the new study section, I was required to invite a group of national authorities to join the group. My boss at the National Institutes of Health, Dr. Murray Goldstein (who later became the director of the National Institute of Neurological Disorders and Stroke) helped me deal with this considerable challenge. With his help, I was able to invite a truly distinguished multidisciplinary group of people to join this new venture. They all agreed to do so.

When we began this work, there were very few applications to review and we took it as our mission to help develop the field. For that reason, we went on site visits very frequently. If a grant proposal looked promising, but inadequate, we went to visit the group to help them do it better. I was on airplanes all the time. It was a truly fascinating experience. At that time, a lot of money was available and we were able to work hard to stimulate much new work in this beginning field. And even as a youngster, I was able to make a difference in what research got funded.

For example, I recall a time during those years when Dr. Lester Breslow of the California Health Department applied to the National Institutes of Health for money to support the establishment of what he called a Human Population Laboratory in Alameda County, California. His idea was to do research in a large representative sample of an entire county over a long period of time to study what he called their health in relation to what he called "way of living." What disease was he going to focus on? None. Instead, he argued that the appropriate outcome for studies of social factors should be "health" and not one or another specific disease. The National Institutes of Health was not sure how to deal with Dr. Breslow's proposal because it did not neatly fit into any of their disease-specific institutes. It turned out that there was no institute at the National Institutes of Health that dealt with health. The NIH deals with heart disease or stroke or diabetes or infectious diseases. Not health. Unfortunately, this is still the case. But that is another story. In any case, I was asked for my advice on how to handle this very unusual application. I suggested that we develop a special study section with a small number of carefully chosen people to deal with this problem case and I was given permission to proceed. To create this special review committee, I invited a few people from my study section to serve, as well as other special outsiders. I attempted to pick people who I thought could understand the radical idea that Dr. Breslow was proposing.

My committee and I went out to California for a two-day meeting with Dr. Breslow. In the end, my meticulously chosen people recommended that the proposal not be funded. His proposal, in the eyes of the committee, was simply too weird. For example, Dr. Breslow proposed to study the health of people, but he was not going to do *one* physical exam or take *any* blood or urine! He was simply going to ask people to rate their own health. I recall he proposed a question that asked "Compared to other people your age, how would you rate your health? Excellent, good, fair, or poor?" This question has turned out to be one of the most powerful predictors of future health in dozens and dozens of studies all over the world, but at that time, it was a very bizarre question indeed. That the Breslow proposal was turned down was very disappointing to me, but I urged Dr. Breslow to resubmit, and a year later, I assembled yet another group of specially picked reviewers to give it another try. And this time it worked. So Dr. Breslow was able to establish this crucial population study that has turned out to be one of the most significant studies in the history of social determinants and disease. A few years later, others were able to establish similar population laboratories in other parts of the country with equally important results.

I recall another research grant application from those early days. Dr. Warren Winkelstein, the man I mentioned earlier as the planner of my retirement party, applied for research funds from the Study Section. He was the first person in the world to request support to study the health effects of air pollution. It was a very clever proposal. He argued that air pollution levels were typically higher in those parts of cities where poor people lived. He also noted that poor people have higher rates of illness than wealthier people. His research was therefore designed to help us figure out whether the cause of disease was due to the air pollution or to economic status. We were all impressed with this creative proposal, but there was no chance that he could be funded based on this cleverness alone. No one had ever heard of this young man. This was his first research project. We therefore decided to go to Buffalo, New York, and meet him in person to discuss his proposal. He was even more impressive when we talked to him in person and he got the grant that launched his distinguished career. Many years later, as a Professor of Epidemiology at the School of Public Health in Berkeley, Warren became the director of one of the first projects in the world to study the epidemiology of AIDS. The AIDS epidemic was just being recognized at that time, and Warren's work established the fundamental knowledge about the disease that has since saved the lives of millions of people.

I did my job with the study section until 1962 when, once again, I handed in my resignation. And once again, I was summoned to the office of the Assistant Surgeon General in Washington who, in an exhausted tone, asked me once again, "Now what? Why are you threatening to resign this time?" My reason for quitting this time was a little unusual. A colleague of mine at the National Institutes of Health wondered if I would be willing to help a friend draft a research grant application. I said I would be happy to do what I could. His friend came and told me his research idea and I began to outline a research grant application based on his ideas. I could soon tell that the plan I was drafting for him had an excellent chance of being funded.

The problem was that I didn't know what he was talking about! He was an ophthalmologist, and he was describing a research project involving retinal pathology that I knew absolutely nothing about. I didn't even know the meaning of many of the words he was using. And yet I was crafting a research grant proposal that I thought had a 90 percent chance of being funded. I had mastered the art of grantsmanship. I could write a successful proposal about anything. This was so offensive to me that I decided, that day, to quit my job. I always had the naive idea that one should win a research grant because of the quality of one's ideas. And here I was, with no ideas at all, writing a successful grant proposal simply because I had an ability to work the system! That was intolerable. It was morally reprehensible. I decided right then to leave and to not send in a research request to the National Institutes of Health for at least ten years so that I would not be able to take advantage of my unfortunate "skill." I just hated the idea of playing this cheating game. It reminded me of my dad in the basement in the middle of the night. "Bring in lots of tools and let's fool this man so that he will pay lots of money." This was another low point in my life.

I didn't tell the Assistant Surgeon General any of this. It was too embarrassing. I told him that the job of being an executive secretary was a wonderful job and that I enjoyed it, but that it was time for me to return to my work as a researcher. It was time for me to actually do research instead of talking about it and reviewing the plans of others. He suggested two possible jobs in the Washington area, but I told him that a job in Washington was likely to involve policy work and consultation duties and that I really just wanted to do research. I told him I thought it was time for me to take a job at a university. He then countered with the idea that a research field station dealing with heart disease could be set up in San Francisco where I could do my research far from the Washington scene. I could see some merit to this idea. Marilyn had been suggesting to me for some time that it would be good for the children to have more contact with their grandparents, who still lived in California. They all lived in the Los Angeles area. Since the new job possibility was in San Francisco, about four hundred miles away, it seemed a safe enough distance for me while it seemed a close enough distance for the grandchildren. I recalled the importance of extended family for me in Winnipeg, and I warmed to the San Francisco possibility.

20

BACK TO CALIFORNIA

In the summer of 1962, we loaded our Peugeot 403 station wagon (along with a bulging roof rack), and with two small children aged three and four in tow, we headed to California for the next chapter. We had no money for hotels, so we camped in a tent every night. This worked reasonably well in nice weather but was a bit of a challenge during all-night rainstorms. I recall one night when our tent was being flooded with water from a particularly heavy storm. We woke the children in the middle of the night, packed the car, and drove to the nearest town: Fargo, North Dakota. The car needed an oil change and, when we happened upon an all-night service station in Fargo, we decided to have that job done at three in the morning. The mechanic hoisted the car on his rack to do the work. To be kind to the children, we allowed them to keep sleeping in the back of the car while it was up in the air. Marilyn and I went across the street to an all-night coffee shop to get some food while we kept an eye on the car. Naturally, the children woke up to find themselves high in the air, in a strange building, without a parent in sight. That took some calming words and some big hugs.

We had taken a northern route to California so that we could visit my family in Winnipeg. We visited my grandmother Gertrude, and she met my wife and children for the first time. We all had dinner together, and everyone enjoyed meeting one another. I happily drove Marilyn and the kids around my old battlegrounds. They cheerfully took it all in, but I was still wincing at some of the memories. A few days later, I drove everyone to Dauphin so that Saul and Harry could meet them too. I also took the kids to Riding Mountain National Park, near Dauphin, so that they could see one of the places that Saul and Harry had taken me as a child. I had told the kids about this park high in the mountains with clear glacial lakes in Northern Manitoba. When we arrived, I realized that my park was at an elevation of perhaps twelve feet. There are no mountains in the Canadian Prairies! But I had not misled them entirely. The water in the lake was really cold. And to be fair, the park is at the fiftieth parallel, and the trees at that latitude are typical of trees that exist at very high mountain elevations. Nevertheless, it was a little embarrassing.

We continued our trip by driving on the Trans-Canada highway to British Columbia and then down the Pacific Coast Highway to California. Camping outdoors every day. Naturally, there we were many adventures along the way. I recall one day when we naively decided to set up our tent so that we sleep at the Oregon seashore. We thought that this would be no problem in the middle of the summer. Little did we know that Oregon summers can be the coldest time of the year. Especially at the seashore! We awoke the first morning frozen and shaken. In discussions with Oregon natives later in the day, they suggested we would enjoy much better weather up in the mountains, just a few miles away. We packed the car and went up the mountain, and we did indeed find a much warmer climate.

During that part of the trip, I also became a hero to my daughter, Karen. She had become enamored with the little chipmunks in the mountains. They were very cute. She spent many hours watching and chasing them. So I decided to catch one for her so that she could take it to our new home in California as a pet. What was I thinking? The boy from the Canadian Prairies was clearly in a world for which he had not been prepared! I worked out a great scheme to succeed in accomplishing my task. I carefully watched a chipmunk hole until one emerged to do his daily chores. I then bent over and covered the hole with a fishing net. After doing this, I got up and frightened the chipmunk so that it raced back to the hole. And there, of course, it got caught in the net and the deed was done. I was a hero! We placed the little guy in a box with air holes and food, and we continued on our way to California.

Coming down from the Oregon mountains turned out to be a challenge. We were all petrified. Driving along, I suddenly noticed an enormous fully loaded logging truck about one foot from my rear bumper. Thinking we were going to be pushed off the curvy road, I pulled off at my first opportunity while the truck swept past us in a gush of wind and with a roaring engine. When my heart rate returned to normal, I pulled onto the road again, and within two minutes, another logging truck was on my bumper. I pulled off again. This calamitous situation repeated itself during the entire chase down the mountain. I was never able to drive as fast as those truck drivers. I learned later that the drivers were paid by the load and people like me were going to send them to the poorhouse.

Later that same day, back on the highway, the engine of our Peugeot station wagon conked out. I called for a tow truck, and the car was delivered to a small garage in a little coastal Oregon town. A very nice mechanic opened the hood to fix the engine but immediately dropped his rag and said, "What is this?" I explained that "this" was a very popular and well-known French car called Peugeot. He said he had never heard of such a thing. He did his best, though, and he was able to contrive a temporary fix that allowed us to continue our journey.

The next day, the adventure continued. We limped into California and were asked to stop at the State of California Inspection Station.

"Are you folks bringing any fruits or vegetables into California?"

"None," we said.

"Any pets or other animals?"

Oops. Karen had to be consoled that the little chipmunk I caught for her would be sent to an even better and more comfortable home where he could have lots of other chipmunk friends and a very nice life.

After three weeks of driving and camping, we crossed the Golden Gate Bridge and entered San Francisco. Just as we approached that glorious bridge, the song playing on the car radio was the majestic Colonel Bogey March. That song had recently been featured in the movie *The Bridge on the River Kwai,* and it would be hard to imagine a more fitting way to triumphantly cross that bridge and enter our new home city after this long and tiring trip. Listen to that glorious tune sometime and visualize our worn-out troop coming to the end of a long journey. I suppose it was just a coincidence?

A month earlier, I had flown out on my own and rented a two-bedroom house one-half block from Golden Gate Park. Our plan was to live in the rented house until we could decide where to buy a house. My job was in the U.S. Public Health Service Hospital, one mile away and near the Golden Gate Bridge. As my Assistant Surgeon General had promised, I could work on any research projects that I wanted. Finally, I thought, my dream had come true! I could do whatever I wanted to do!

21

FINAL YEARS IN THE GOVERNMENT

I returned to the puzzle of coronary heart disease. It was the number 1 cause of death in the United States, and we were just then beginning to develop some ideas about its causes and about ways to possibly prevent it. My interest continued to be on the social factors that increased the risk. Because of the research we had stimulated at the study section at the National Institutes of Health, it was becoming clear that a field of research in social epidemiology was emerging. This research was not of very high quality, nor were the results compelling, but some interesting questions were beginning to emerge.

I had a conversation with a friend at UCLA, Professor Leo Reeder, about this developing field of research, and we decided it might be a good idea to bring together all the people in the country who were engaged in this research to share what we were all doing and to think about next steps. Leo was a professor in the Department of Behavioral Sciences at UCLA who was studying the health consequences of overwork. He had no money for organizing such a meeting. On the other hand, I was a government employee with a better potential for finding such money, and I prevailed upon my bosses in the Public Health Service to provide funds for this purpose. They agreed, and the conference (called "The Social Epidemiology of Coronary Heart Disease") was held in Phoenix, Arizona. We invited all of the social scientists and medical people in the country doing research on heart disease as well as some others who, while they were not doing such research, were nevertheless bright and potentially helpful. We scoured the country and came up with twenty-seven people, including Reeder and myself.

The report of our conference was later published in April 1967 as a special volume of the *Milbank Memorial Quarterly* with the title "Social Stress and Cardiovascular Disease." It is a little embarrassing to read the book now and see the state of the art at that time, but it was quite clear that, in spite of our fumbling early efforts, something important was happening. I wrote a chapter in that book that was based on the idea proposed by Lester Breslow in the Alameda County Study. That paper, written many years ago, is still the centerpiece of my work and thinking today. It argued that we need a new conceptual model, a new way of classifying disease if we are going to successfully develop effective programs to prevent disease. That new model would move away from a clinical classification of disease (heart disease, cancer, arthritis) to a socio-environmental classification (stress, poverty, hope).

Bringing up the name of Leo Reeder has caused me some difficulty. My writing of this memoir suddenly deteriorated. The reason for my distress: On September 25, 1978, I was scheduled to give a talk in San Diego, California, when, the evening before, I received a call from Washington that required my attendance there the next day. I called my friend Leo Reeder in Los Angeles and asked if he could attend the San Diego meeting in my place. He readily agreed. When my plane landed in Washington on the twenty-fifth, I saw newspaper headlines that a plane had crashed while attempting to land at the San Diego airport. It had collided with a small Cessna airplane. Leo had been a passenger on Pacific Southwest Airlines Flight 182. That crash remains the deadliest aircraft disaster in California history. On the plane itself, 135 died. Including my friend Leo. The two men aboard the Cessna died, as did seven people on the ground, including a family of four. Nine others on the ground were injured and twenty-two homes were destroyed or damaged. Leo left behind his wife, Sharon, and two children. Sharon later asked me to be a godfather to their youngest child. I haven't fully recovered from that trauma even now, over thirty years later.

I continued working at the Public Health Service Hospital in San Francisco doing the research I wanted to do until everything changed, once again. My friend Dr. Paul Ehrlich had been chief of the San Francisco research station, and his presence allowed me to do as I pleased. Then, suddenly, Paul was transferred back to Washington to take on a new, very challenging assignment: Assistant Surgeon General for International Health. Who could possibly take his place? The answer was obvious. Me. This was exactly what I was trying to avoid. I had, by then, begun regular meetings with one of the smartest men I have ever known. Reuell Stallones was a professor of epidemiology at the School of Public Health in Berkeley. He had an MD degree and had previously been a parachuting physician in the Marine Corps. He is one of the few people I have ever known who made my wild and crazy ideas seem mild and pedestrian. He was always one step ahead of me. I had been meeting with Stallones for some months by then with the request that he help me to identify the most important ideas in the field of coronary heart disease. I was not interested in discussing anything conventional and normal. We spent months and months filling up chalkboards with ideas and concepts and circles and arrows and finally came up with a research idea that would change everything. At least that's what we thought.

Our idea was to study coronary heart disease among Japanese men who had migrated from Japan to Hawaii or to the San Francisco Bay Area. This was an interesting project because the Japanese in Japan had the lowest rate of coronary heart disease in the world (they still do), and no one knew why. One hypothesis was that they were protected by good genes. Another was that they ate a very low-fat diet. My hypothesis concerned their social and cultural patterns. Stallones and I applied for research funds to do this project. It was a massive undertaking. We planned to study 18,000 Japanese men living in three geographic locations using the most elaborate and sophisticated research tools then available. Happily, review groups at the National Institutes of Health approved our very expensive request for funds and, in 1966, we began our work.

Doing this research involved my traveling to Japan on several occasions. During an evening on one of those trips, I had been taken to a nightclub where I was invited to try a new gadget. It was called karaoke. Karaoke had just been invented by the Japanese musician Daisuke Inoue. The karaoke device allows amateurs to sing along with recorded music by using a microphone and speaker system. Lyrics are projected on a screen to assist the singer. I was given a list of hundreds of songs to choose from and, without even thinking about it, I chose "I Did It My Way."

When I learned that Paul was leaving and going back to Washington, I told Stallones that I was dreading becoming the chief of the research field station. In response to this, he somehow convinced the university that I should be recruited to join the faculty at Berkeley. The university reviewed my record and solicited dozens of letters from all over the world to determine my worth, and in 1968, they created a new faculty position for me. I accepted that offer and joined the faculty of the School of Public Health as a tenured full professor of epidemiology. It turns out that I was the first sociologist in the world ever to be appointed to a department of epidemiology. This was the real beginning of the field of social epidemiology. I later received a very large grant from the National Institutes of Health to begin a training program to recruit and train young people in this new field and that grant was renewed every year for the next twenty-five years. That grant trained most of the leaders in social epidemiology in the world today.

Full professor, Berkeley, 1968

By that time, 1968, Marilyn and I had our third child, Janet. She was born in August 1963. Because of my new job in Berkeley, we moved from San Francisco to a new house in Orinda, California, near Berkeley. As I mentioned earlier, I have remained in my job as a professor for forty-three years now. After my history of resigning from job after job, it's interesting that I have stayed put in this job. There are several reasons for this turnaround. First, I have been able to do whatever I have wanted to do, without any restrictions. I have been able to build a field that now has worldwide presence. Second, I have been able to help guide a new generation of young people to move this work forward. Third, I have been able to do this work without telling lies, without pretending, and without practicing gamesmanship. And fourth, as best I can tell, I have been able to make a difference.

22

THE UNIVERSITY OF CALIFORNIA AT BERKELEY

The goal of the research I have done has been to understand why some people are less healthy than others. And why some people maintain good health in spite of disadvantages. When I came to the University in Berkeley, I was really able to pursue these questions in the way that I had wanted to: nonstop with full-out energy. I studied the health of San Francisco bus drivers; Japanese migrants; civil service workers in England; people living in public housing in Belgrade, Yugoslavia; older people living in a retirement community; and American men at very high risk of developing coronary heart disease. In all of this work, it has turned out that there is much more involved in answering these questions than good genes, good medical care, and a healthy lifestyle. The findings from this research clearly show that the social environments in which people live has a major influence on health.

There is, of course, more to it than that. When we attempt to intervene to help improve the health of people, we need to be mindful of the importance of the social environment as well. A focus on the usual risk factors—serum cholesterol, high blood pressure, cigarette smoking, obesity—that does not take into account the fundamental societal forces that influence those risk factors is doomed to failure.

I once wrote about this in one of my papers and it has been has been quoted by many people in many places: "Even as we intervene on the risk factors we *do* know about, new people enter the at-risk population because we have done nothing to influence those forces in our society that caused the problems in the first place."

It is only now, many years after I have done this work, that I can see that my early years in Winnipeg motivated me to pursue these projects. That a person's early years have an influence on one's later life is hardly worthy of comment. Of course that is true. From my early experiences in the North End of Winnipeg, however, I came away with the conviction that a challenging environment can either ruin your life or it can provide a motivation to escape. The question in my mind has been to help identify some of the factors that move things in one direction or the other.

The power of early environments on later life, success or failure, is illustrated in the classic work of Betty Hart and Todd Risley. In 1995, these researchers studied three income categories of families: professional, working class, and welfare. They did intensive research in the homes of these families over a long period of time and found that children in welfare families heard an average of 616 words per hour while children from professional families heard an average of 2,153 words per hour. Hart and Risley calculated that this resulted in a 30 million-word gap between these children by the time they were three years old! Children from working class families were in between. It turned out that lower word counts early in life dramatically affected the ability of these children to listen and read and understand when they were ten years old. And you can be certain that these differences continue to have an impact on the lives of these kids throughout their lives.

But while early life is clearly important, early life disadvantages don't necessarily mean you are doomed. If my memoir has a central message, I hope that this is it. The Hart and Risley scores are averages. Some kids do even worse than the average but some kids are able to overcome these early life challenges and do much better than the average.

The role of early life was a central influence in my early research work. It is even more important in my current work. The main question in my current work is one I have already mentioned several times: why do people who are better off, people who are in higher social classes, have better health than poor people? Everyone in public health knows that this is the major question. It is the subject of the first lecture in schools of public health, and it is discussed in the first chapter in virtually every public health textbook. The question is, why does this happen? Is it because people in lower social class positions are poor? Is that really the issue? Or is that poor people don't have good medical care? Or is it because they don't have good educations? Or that they have bad housing? Unsafe jobs? The answer is that it is probably a combination of all of these things.

Since we don't have a clear answer to this question, no one knows what can be done to help people in lower social class positions. Social class divisions have always been with us, and short of revolution, it is not likely that we can make them disappear. This has been very frustrating for those of us committed to helping build a healthy society. One of the most important determinants of health, social class, is something we knew we could do nothing about. It has been the elephant in the room that no one talks about.

Then, in 1991, there was a breakthrough on this problem. A former student of mine, Michael Marmot, made a remarkable discovery while studying the health of ten thousand British civil servants. Michael had been my student at Berkeley when I was doing the study of Japanese migrants. He did his Ph.D. dissertation on the Japanese project and he was clearly an outstanding young man. The reason he came to Berkeley in the first place is interesting: I was giving a lecture in New Zealand in 1973 describing the work we were doing at Berkeley in the new field of social epidemiology. At the end of my lecture, Dr. Peter Harvey introduced himself to me. He said, "I am a Professor of Medicine at the University of Sydney. Do you really do this research at Berkeley?" I said we did. He then said, "We have a student in our medical school who is driving us crazy. He questions everything we teach him. What he wants to do is the kind of work now going on at Berkeley. He is the best student in our school, but unfortunately, I think he would be much happier with you than with us. When he graduates with his MD degree next month, would you accept him into your Ph.D. program if we gave him a fellowship?" I said, "Yes!"

So Michael Marmot and his architect wife, Alexi, came to Berkeley to begin his truly remarkable career in Social Epidemiology. He is the only student I have had who is now a knight. He is Professor Sir Michael Marmot. But he still permits me to call him "Michael." Anyway, in his study of the civil servants, Michael observed what we always observe: those in the lower civil service ranks (guards, deliverymen) had rates of coronary heart disease four times higher than those civil servants at the top. And this difference could not be explained by differences in the usual heart disease risk factors such as serum cholesterol levels, hypertension, or cigarette smoking. And all of the people in England have good medical care because of their National Health Service. That research finding was not new. That's always what we find.

Then Michael reported something none of us had ever seen before. There was a gradient in disease by social class ranking. Those civil servants at the top of occupational hierarchy had low rates of disease but those one step below them, professionals and executives, doctors, and lawyers, had rates of disease twice as high as those at the very top. These professionals and executives were not poor, they didn't have poor educations, they didn't live in poor neighborhoods, and yet their rates were higher than those one step above them. And there was a progressive stepwise gradient in disease rates from top to bottom of the social class ladder. While people at the bottom did have the highest rates, and while this should not be ignored, the fact that people even near the top had high rates as well suggests that something else was going on to explain the link between social class ranking and disease, something else in addition to money, education, housing, jobs, and medical care. What could that "something else" be?

Michael then reported that he found the same thing when he looked not just at coronary heart disease but when he looked at all diseases. I was in London with him when he made this discovery. When I got back to Berkeley, a group of us checked to see if Michael's finding was limited to British civil servants. We checked the data from every industrialized country in the world and for all diseases, and we found exactly the same thing as he found in London!

So being in a lower social class position was not the issue. What could explain higher disease rates even near the top of the social class hierarchy? The hypothesis I suggested to explain this finding is now being confirmed by many others. I suggested that the explanation was "control of destiny." By that phrase, I meant the ability of people to deal with the issues that confront them in their daily lives. I suggested that those at the top of the civil service hierarchy (they are the people who wear black bowler hats and striped pants and who carry umbrellas and who rule everything in their world) have the best ability to deal with life issues and that this ability lessens progressively as one goes down the social class ladder. We now have evidence that having less control affects immune functioning in the body. The less control a person has, the weaker that person's bodily defense systems. The weaker a person's defense systems, the more vulnerable that person is to such disease risk factors as viruses, air pollution, and stress. The more vulnerable a person is to disease risk factors, the higher the rate of disease will be.

This seemingly obvious model of disease causation has for many years been widely understood and accepted by epidemiologists who study infectious diseases. They know that disease agents such as viruses and bacteria affect people only when people have weakened defense systems and are vulnerable to them. But epidemiologists who study such noninfectious diseases as heart disease, cancer, and arthritis have not looked at diseases in that way. Our focus has been more on disease risk factors and not on host susceptibility. If, for example, you are told that you have a high cholesterol level, your doctor is likely to advise that you lower it. If you smoke cigarettes, you will be advised to stop. Those are good things to do. But our research is now showing that all the risk factors we know about account for less than half the disease that occurs. These risk factors we already know about are important, but there are other forces at play as well, and they need to be taken into account as well. Those "other forces" include host susceptibility. And it is turning out that host susceptibility is a major influence in affecting people's ability to control the events that impinge on their lives. Being exposed to risk factors is one thing. Being vulnerable to them is something else.

As I mentioned earlier, I am now co-director of the Berkeley Health Care for Action Center. Everything we do in the Center is directed toward helping people to deal with difficult challenges in their lives. We have projects to help parents do a better job with their children, to help poor people manage their lives in spite of their poverty, to help people with disabilities function in an unfair world, to help people without resources to better manage their medical treatment after they leave the hospital, and to help people of low literacy better understand medical instructions and drug labels.

Having control of the events in my life has always been my goal. Hang a shingle and do your own thing. Escape from the restricted residential ghetto, avoid the crowds, and help people who are being treated unfairly. While having control has been one of my personal goals, I would go so far as to suggest that this idea might be important for many people as well. The evidence certainly is now showing that having this kind of control over life events can have helpful consequences for health.

When I mention this idea of control in my classes at Berkeley, I notice that most students merely nod agreeably. My guess is that most don't really know what I am talking about. My sense is that most of these students learned from their parents very early in life that there are many ways to solve problems. If you can't do things one way, there are other ways to do it. You don't get admitted to Berkeley if you haven't mastered that idea. When I interview poor people, however, I see an entirely different world. When these poor people are told that they can't solve a problem because there is a rule against the thing they want to do, you can see their shoulders slump. Defeated again. No way to work things out. And it's not that they are deficient in intelligence or creativity. It's that they have been trained from their earliest days that you cannot fight the rules. You can't win against the authorities. In our work with them, you can see the lights go on in their eyes when we show them a variety of actual alternatives for dealing with their problems. Over time, they really get it. You don't have to accept a "no." There *are* things that can be done. Growing up in the North End really has had a major impact on my work. It affects my thinking daily. I am convinced about the power of being able to control one's destiny. It is critical for health and well-being. In fact, much of my career work has been centered on this idea.

Consider for example, our work with San Francisco bus drivers. Their health status is not good. They have high rates of hypertension, back pain, respiratory distress, gastrointestinal difficulties, and alcohol problems. Without going into all the details, let me just say that almost all of their health problems are a result of work stress. Drivers must keep to a schedule that can never be met and they are punished when they are late. But they are always late because the schedule cannot possibly be met. You would think that the bus schedule would be developed by driving from bus stop to bus stop and noting how long that takes. Instead, in San Francisco, there are not enough buses and the bus schedule is made by a computer that allocates times based on the number of buses that are available, not on how long the routes actually take. Drivers are therefore always late. The drivers attempt to compensate for this by giving up rest stops at the end of the line and zipping into fast food restaurants along the way to use the bathroom or to get food. Because they are always late, passengers are often angry with the drivers. Drivers are often then impolite to passengers because they feel they are being blamed for a situation that is not in their control. Passengers then get upset because drivers are impolite. This job circumstance is unfair to all, and it has health consequences. It is helpful for people to control the events that impinge on their lives and there are often serious consequences when that cannot be done. Again, without my being consciously aware of it, my research on bus drivers was influenced by my early days in Winnipeg. It is better to be able to control the events that impinge on your life.

This account of some of my research suggests that I have been a major force in this work. That would be a big exaggeration. Many people credit me with significant work on the importance of social support for health, on the importance of socioeconomic status as a determinant of health, on the role of control, on the need to redefine our focus on fundamental determinants of health instead of on clinical conditions, and so on. I did work on these issues, but all of these ideas, to a greater or lesser degree, came from my students. I am not that smart. What I am good at is picking students brighter than I am, encouraging them to go beyond what they think they are capable of, helping them to navigate a sometimes challenging science world, and ensuring that they get lots of credit and recognition.

For example, when Lisa Berkman was a Ph.D. student at Berkeley, she was the one who suggested that we do research on the health consequences of social isolation. I was her thesis supervisor and a co-author of our paper on social support, but she was the one who thought up the project, she did the analysis, and she did the writing. Once again, I was only helping as she developed a completely new line of research. The paper we wrote is now one of the most widely referenced pieces in the literature. What some call a classic. It is her work, not mine. Lisa is now a distinguished professor at Harvard and one of the leading scholars in the world in social epidemiology.

I want to emphasize that my advising work with students is not simply a result of my being a wonderful and generous person. I behave in this way because my students really are smarter than I am and I am the one taking advantage of them. Not the other way around. To my credit, however, I am a good picker. I have picked a student out of a group of many, knowing that particular person is special, when others might not have seen the potential. I have done this my entire professional life, and I rarely have been wrong. Unfortunately, I don't know how I do this. I wish I could manufacture a list of qualities I look for, but that list would be artificial and I will not play that game. Hundreds of former students have communicated to me in one way or another that I changed their lives. I appreciate that. What these students don't know is that they changed my life even more. I have won all kinds of awards and been rewarded in many ways when, in my opinion, my main contribution has been to hang on to the coattails of my students. They deserve the awards.

23

BUT WAIT, THERE'S MORE!

Throughout my story, I have tried to figure out how I was able to grow up in a challenging family and neighborhood and end up being able to help make the world a better place. I have described several factors that I thought were important in allowing this to happen for me. These factors are:

1. The need to escape (being beaten up)
2. Feeling like a worthwhile person (in spite of everything)
3. Working hard (on every job and assignment)
4. Being a good boy (even when I hated it)
5. Having a safe place to dream (with Andrew Carnegie on my side)
6. Having a good education (with my Oxford in the prairies) and
7. Learning to avoid interpersonal dangers (navigating challenging interpersonal situations and playing well with others).

As they say on late night television, "but wait, there's more!" Underlying everything I have said is another factor that underlies all these things and that, in my view, is essential to everything. (And I came up with this idea before President Barack Obama made it popular!) The idea I am referring to is a factor called Hope. If I didn't have a sense that I had a future out there somewhere, I think that none of the factors I have just mentioned would have had any importance. Hope, in my view, is the foundation for everything.

I have always felt this way. But my feelings were vague and ill-formed. Without recognizing the idea, hope was the basis for my work on religion in the Seventh-day Adventist study and it certainly influenced my thinking about control of destiny in the civil service project. But in 2001, a doctoral student and I began to talk really seriously and specifically about it and we actually submitted a research grant application to study the concept of hope. That student, Nance Wilson, was beginning to think about doing a doctoral thesis about the difficulties that very poor, young people have in surviving their challenging worlds. She had herself grown up in poverty and the idea she was working on grew out of her that experience. As part of her preparation, she brought to my attention an announcement from the Centers of Disease Control and Prevention of the U.S. Public Health Service. The CDC wanted to support innovative research on problems that affected youth: cigarette smoking and drug use, violence, poor school performance, and inappropriate sexual behavior. Nance and I decided to send in an application to compete for these funds. If we were successful, this money would allow her to complete her doctoral studies. (A challenge facing professors in research universities is to come up with funds to support the research of their doctoral students. I have spent much of my professorial life in the very competitive world of fundraising for such purposes. This has not been one of my favorite activities.)

Nance came up with a wonderful plan. She had been working with fifth grade children in Richmond, California. Richmond is a very low-income city about five miles north of Berkeley. Unemployment rates are very high there. So are crime rates. Especially murder rates. The city is also plagued by heavy air pollution from nearby oil refineries. Richmond used to be a sleepy little town until the beginning of the Second World War. Shortly after the United States got into that war, it became apparent that the United States did not have enough ships to transport troops and supplies to Europe and Henry Kaiser built an enormous ship building facility in Richmond to meet that need. In response, thousands of people migrated to Richmond, mostly people from the Southern regions of the U.S., to work in the shipyards. Soon after the war, the shipyard closed and left the people in Richmond without jobs. Years later, the consequence of that history is now visible on nearly every street in the city.

The main thing that Nance learned in her interviews with these fifth graders was that many of them did not think they would live beyond the age of twenty. In our research proposal to the CDC, we therefore said that we were not going to study any of the topics they suggested. We were not going to design a project around cigarette smoking and drug use, or around violence, or around poor school performance, or inappropriate sexual behavior. This decision to ignore the rules of the granting agency, by the way, is not one I recommend for getting a research grant. Instead, we said we were going to focus on hope. We came to that conclusion because of the finding that so many kids knew they would not live beyond twenty. We said to CDC that since so many of these kids had no hope for the future, it just didn't matter to them whether or not they smoked or did well in school. The CDC received several hundred research grant applications and, amazingly, they chose ours as the number 1 project in the country. Even though we didn't follow their rules.

After receiving funds to do this work, Nance did a wonderful job and wrote a brilliant Ph.D. thesis describing her work with these children. What she did with them was compelling. She worked with small groups of them in several schools in Richmond. She gave each child a camera and film and showed them how to use it. (This is a technique first developed a few years earlier by another student at Berkeley called Photovoice.) The children went out into the school and into their community and took pictures of the things that bothered them about their world. The children in each group then spent hours and hours discussing their pictures to decide which projects they would work on. One group, for example, chose to clean up the graffiti that had overwhelmed their school. We then helped them work out a project plan to make their dream come true. You can't just go out to the hardware store, buy paint and brushes, and go to work. You have to develop a work strategy. You have to request permission from the appropriate school authorities and you have to structure your request appropriately. And so on. Each group of children learned that you can have a dream but they also learned that you need to work in special ways to make your dream come true. All of this was intended to teach a child that you can have hope in your life.

I want to emphasize one point by telling this story: without hope, nothing else we do matters. Sitting and reading in the Carnegie library is an inspiring activity only if, at some level, you know that you can have a future. What would the library experience be like if you were without hope? Or what you would derive from John Milton's poem regarding Heav'n and Hell if you felt nothing mattered anyway? So in my thinking, hope is the indispensable force that makes everything else come alive. The question then becomes how can we help people, but especially kids, see that they can have hope? Here is where the factors I have mentioned above come into play. For me, each of these seven experiences, by themselves, stimulated the beginnings of hope in my mind but each of them interacted with the others so that, in the end, I became convinced that I could have a future. I left the North End with my head held high.

I recently received a major grant from the Robert Wood Johnson Foundation to further explore these issues. These ideas are not the normal ones that are usually funded; it is no coincidence that the division of the Foundation that approved our funding is called the "Pioneering Ideas Program." Our research focuses on the very poor people who live in two wards in Las Vegas, Nevada. Most of the people living in Wards 3 and 5 are immigrants who came to this country so that their children could have a better life than they have had. Most of them work in the kitchens or in the room cleaning crews of the major hotels and casinos in Las Vegas. In this project, we hope to show that the ideas discussed here really do make a difference—that children living in challenging circumstances can develop a sense of hope and that they can find ways to have satisfying and rewarding lives.

24

MY CHILDREN

As I have indicated at different places in this memoir, Marilyn and I had three children. Karen was born in 1958, David in 1959, and Janet in 1963. All three of these children are now successful and happy adults. Karen and Janet are married to great men (Steve and Greg respectively) and they each have two children (Nolan and Jenna with Karen and Steve and Christopher and Melanie with Janet and Greg). I would love to take some credit for the way these three kids turned out, but that would be a wild exaggeration. The truth is that while the children were growing up, I was either working or I was on an airplane traveling the world to work somewhere else. I have a membership card for admission to the United Airlines Red Carpet Club that is a sort of grim testimony to my traveling claim. The current annual fee for membership in the club is $450. United also used to offer a lifetime membership that cost several thousands of dollars. I received a lifetime membership card, for free. This was not because I am such a nice guy but because I was one of United's very best customers. Instead of reading nursery rhymes to the kids and taking them to the park, I was getting on and off airplanes.

If I wasn't on an airplane, I was working. I was either hard at work in Berkeley or at home, but I was always working. The Adelman twins would probably have been sitting around having a soda or having fun in some other way while I was slaving away. Just like in Winnipeg, twenty years earlier. I worked every evening until late and I worked almost all weekends. As a consequence, I never told my children stories, or sang to them, or read to them. I wouldn't have done it well anyway. As I have indicated more than once, my mother never read to me the books that most children know and I never got the chance to read those books to my children.

My daughter, Karen, read the above paragraph and wrote me a note, "Dad, I think you shouldn't be so critical. You read *Chitty Chitty Bang Bang* to us, and I remember every second of it. You sang cowboy songs in the car. You told us stories at the dinner table and offered us a nickel if we knew the answers to your fun questions. You weren't engaged the way you think you should have been, but you were a presence with quality if not quantity."

There was one time during those years when I was actually the kind of father I thought I should be. In 1975, I was able to take a sabbatical year. I could take an entire year off to do whatever I wanted, wherever I wanted. Marilyn and I were conscious of the fact that the children were still attending school and we decided that we could only go to a country where English was the spoken language. After some letter writing, we decided to go to England for the year. I was offered a position at York University in England. I would be a Visiting Scholar in the Institute of Social and Economic Studies with the understanding that I would not be expected to do any teaching or perform any other duties. The Department of Health Economics at York was one of the foremost units in the world at that time, and it still is. We were offered housing on the campus. We were told that the school system in York was excellent and that our children would be welcome. Karen was in the twelfth grade, David was in the eleventh grade, and Janet was in the seventh grade.

I decided that if we were all going to travel to Europe, and live there for a year, we might as well take full advantage of this situation and do some touring as well. To do that, I thought we would need a car. So I visited the Mercedes dealer in Walnut Creek, California, and arranged to buy a Mercedes 300 Diesel that we could pick up and use in Europe and then ship home at the end of the year. I learned a week later that the car would not be available for pickup until November 1. We would land in Europe in July. Not to be done in by this little inconvenience, I decided to also buy a tiny car that we could pick up in July and that we could use in the interim.

As a family, we developed a brilliant battle plan to accomplish this mission. All five of us would visit car dealerships that sold little cars available in four designated countries: England, France, Germany, and Italy. We each brought along an empty suitcase that we loaded into the test cars. We then squeezed our bodies into the cars. The only car that could accommodate this invasion was a little Fiat sedan. So I bought that car as well and arranged to pick it up near Milan in July.

We did tour Italy from top to bottom (Florence, the Vatican, Pompeii) and we also traveled through Germany, Switzerland, Austria, the Netherlands (Anne Frank's house), and France. At the end of August, we drove our little car onto a ferryboat and arrived, finally, in England.

Obviously, I was with the family every day during that adventure. No work, no phone calls, no meetings. My daily presence in family affairs actually continued through most of that year. Marilyn spent most of her time out of the house exploring various philosophical and spiritual traditions in

England while I did the cooking, shopping, and laundry. These tasks were not as easily done as one might imagine. I learned to shop daily for groceries along with other Yorkshire Mums: vegetables in one shop, meat purchases in several other shops, and fancy, exotic foods (like coffee beans) in yet another shop. It was an exciting time. For example, I recall driving down a particular street in York where, every day, I noticed a long line of women at Scotts, The Pork Butcher. Not wanting to miss out, I got in line too and, when I eventually got to the counter, the butcher asked me what I would like. I said, "I don't know. What are all these women buying?" I was told they were buying pork loins. I said, "That's what I want too." Then, of course, I had to figure out how to cook them. But I did become reasonably good at cooking. Not all went well. Shopping and cooking was fraught with many challenges. One day, I tried to make Yorkshire pudding to accompany my roast beef. Unfortunately, the pastry failed to rise. Instead of nice, fluffy confections, my creations were little, flat, oval objects. The family decided to call my product "Yorkshire pudlettes." I was also a strict taskmaster. I recall buying bananas and insisting that everyone eat them before they turned brown. They turned brown anyway. I learned to make banana bread.

As Thanksgiving approached that year, I began planning for a dinner to which we would invite other Americans living in York. I went to my meat butcher and was told that there was no such thing as a turkey available. I was told to try my "exotic" store. They had no idea of what I was talking about either. But, together, we worked out a way to order an outrageously expensive turkey that could be shipped from America. Cranberry sauce? "What are you talking about, sir?" But that could be shipped too. In the end, I received all the ingredients I needed, but two problems emerged. First, so many people said they wanted to come to our dinner that I had to prevail on one of our American friends to have the dinner at her house. Our house was too small to accommodate everyone. Second, the big American turkey was too large to fit into the tiny little oven available to us in England in those days. (We used brute force and succeeded in getting the turkey into the tiny space anyway.)

I learned to do the laundry. That was not easy either. I had to drive a mile or so to a coin-operated laundry where, for the first time in my life, I learned to buy the proper soap, load the washing machines with whites and colors *separately*, dry the washed clothing, and finally, and most difficult, neatly fold everything while I was *still* in the laundry shop. Not at home.

I took the kids to and from school every day and was around to help them with homework and with after-school snacks.

One of the highlights of my time in York was that I was able to spend more time with Janet. The older kids were off with their friends, and Janet and I became good travel buddies. I wanted to travel around the York area, but my lack of skill in navigation was a serious limitation. Janet, on the other hand, was a whiz with maps and directions. She was only twelve years old at the time, but she was really good at the job. We traveled down little unmarked lanes all over Yorkshire, and she kept us on track every time. We visited Haworth, the home of the Bronte sisters. We visited the Moors. We visited prehistoric burial sites. During the spring months, we toured the countryside to see the world's most beautiful daffodils in full bloom. So while I complain about my absence as a father, there were a few times when I was able to do a pretty good job.

My evolution continued after Karen had her first baby. After Nolan was born in 1995, I bravely volunteered to take on the responsibility that Marilyn normally would have done. But Marilyn was recovering from an automobile accident, and so I said, "I'll do it!" I slept on a sofa bed at Karen's house. I did the cooking, I changed the diapers, and I did other helpful things. I didn't do any of them very well because, other than my cooking expertise, I had no experience at all. But I certainly was eager and enthusiastic!

Later, when Nolan and his new sister, Jenna, were older, I happily babysat with them every Monday. I told astonished people at work that I was not going to be in the office on Mondays! On that day, the kids and I went on adventures. We would go to the Lawrence Hall of Science. This building is located high in the Berkeley hills overlooking the university. It is set up specifically for young people. You can build things out of blocks, you can do little science experiments, and you can play games. At other times, we would go to the Exploratorium in San Francisco where you can do even more science-oriented things. We would sometimes go the movies. One day we went to the recycling center where we could see what happens to bottles and newspapers after they have been picked up at people's homes. We went to Buchanan Airfield and watched airplanes take off and land. We went to different playgrounds. And we always ate interesting lunches at different places around the area. These were some of the best times I have had in my life.

Lunch with my grandson Nolan

In the early days, I would pick the kids up at around 11:00 a.m. and we would not get home until 5:00 p.m. or so. When they began school, I would pick them up as their school day ended (perhaps at noon, 1:00 p.m., 2:00 p.m.), and we would then go off to explore. As the children advanced into higher grades and their school days got longer, our time together became more and more limited. Eventually, I had to let go of our fun time together. The kids had other things to do. Like taking music lessons, working with tutors, and other important activities such as playing with their friends. I knew the day would eventually come when I was no longer needed, but it was still a rude shock. Happily, however, the kids and I really bonded during our "Monday" times and we are still best buddies, even though I was cast aside.

A challenging part of babysitting involved my total inadequacy as a storyteller. I didn't know any the stories that many children know. What was it with those three little pigs and that wolf? What did people mean when they said that one little piggy went to the market but another one stayed home?

Who was Goldilocks? And why, in the evening, will a kid look into the darkening sky and suddenly shout out "Star light, star bright"!? As I became a babysitter for my grandchildren, my deprived childhood suddenly hit me full force. I was really distressed. I solved this little problem in the same way I dealt with my problems in Winnipeg. I went to the Walnut Creek City Library. I must have been an interesting sight. An older man sitting on a little stool in the children's section day after day reading all the children's books that he could find. I did all of Grimm's fairy tales, and Hans Christian Andersen, Robert Louis Stevenson, and on and on. I actually became quite good at it. Then I could read these books to my grandchildren with confidence and I could have a question and answer session with them and I could hold my head high. No grades of B for me!

Reading to my granddaughter Jenna

But when my own children were growing up, I did none of those things. Marilyn did all the work and she did it brilliantly. I had basically abandoned her with three little kids while I worked nonstop with full intensity at several research jobs. When I have told others about this failure to be a good father, they, like Karen before them, have rushed to my defense. They say that the '50s and '60s were a different time. I shouldn't blame myself for being part of that era. Role models depicting family life in those days were strongly influenced by Ward and June Cleaver in the popular TV show *Leave it to Beaver* and by Robert Young in the equally popular show *Father Knows Best*. In these All-American feel-good family sitcoms, fathers were the breadwinners and mothers stayed at home and looked after the children. For many years, I convinced myself that the "different era" excuse did explain my absence from family life. But in reality, underneath it all, I never really accepted that lame excuse. Based on my experiences as a kid in Winnipeg, I knew that I needed to play an important role in the lives of my children and, while the "different era" excuse is comforting, it was never an acceptable explanation for my behavior. I should have done better.

Why was I so busy? I was furiously trying to earn enough money to keep the family going, and I was madly trying to do a great job in my work. What was I doing at work that kept me so busy? One thing I was doing was developing a brand-new curriculum in the new field of social epidemiology. That had never been done before, anywhere in the world. So I taught new classes for the first time. And I worked for over a year to develop the training grant proposal that I then submitted to the National Institutes of Health. This was to get fellowship money for outstanding students to work with me in this new field. As I mentioned earlier, I got that grant and held it for twenty-five years—one of the longest running training grants in the history of the National Institute of Health. It deeply pleases me that this grant was responsible for training a whole new generation of people all over the world who now have developed the field of social epidemiology.

In addition to my teaching work, I was working on two or three separate research projects simultaneously. Directing one research project is to be expected. Doing two or three at the same time is a recipe for disaster! I did that for over thirty years. And I advised dozens and dozens of doctoral students. Again, three or four students during an academic year is a very big, but doable, job. More than that is crazy-making. And I was on lots of committees. As I mentioned earlier, I was even chairman of a department at the School of Public Health for seven long years! And it was a big department, with two hundred faculty and staff members and hundreds of students.

By the time I got home in those days, I stumbled directly into my study with a cocktail, shut the door, and tried to redeem my sanity. I often talked to no one. I just stared at the wall. I'm sure that neither Marilyn nor the kids had any idea of why Dad didn't talk to them. Had they done something to offend? Was there something they could do to make amends? Did I not love them anymore?

I look back at those times with sadness. But here is the embarrassing, painful and terrible thing about all this: if I had it to do all over again, knowing what I know now, would I have done things differently? I am anguished about this, but I think the honest answer is "no." I would do the same things as I did then. How can I possibly say this? The answer, I think, is that my drive to achieve, to make a difference, to be seen as not useless, is so strong that it trumps everything else. I can't defend this attitude. In fact, I am distressed by it. This is not the kind of person I would like to be. But there I am.

One resolution I made about being a father, however, was even more important to me than these other things. I resolved that if I had a son, I was not going to treat him as my father had treated me. I remember as if it were yesterday the day that pregnant Marilyn and I walked to our local ice cream shop in New Haven to talk about our new baby. I told Marilyn that if we had a boy, I was really going to need her help. If she saw me treating my son the way my father treated me, she was not to let it pass. I pleaded with her to help me not let this happen. And I never did behave that way to David. I was wonderful. I always complimented, supported, and praised him. I never challenged him with bottle caps and I went out of my way to make sure that almost every one of his reasonable wishes was tended to as best I was able to do.

A few years ago, David and I were talking about our relationship during his youth and I told him how proud I was that I avoided behaving like my father. "I don't think," I said, "that I ever criticized you even once while you were growing up." He almost fell to floor laughing.

"You're not serious, are you?" he said.

I was stunned. Of course I was serious! He then gently explained how things really were. He said, "Suppose you are playing tennis with Pete Sampras. He hits the ball to you, and you return the shot, but it goes into the stands. And Pete says, 'Good shot!'"

David then said, "You're right, Dad. Pete Sampras was not criticizing me for my terrible shot into the stands, but Pete and I both knew it wasn't a great shot, didn't we? Do you think I wasn't aware of my screw-ups just because you didn't say anything critical?" Oh my . . .

In spite of the fact that I was an absent father, my relationship with my children these days is outstanding. I love them, I admire them, I respect them, and best of all, they have all become much better human beings than I could ever dream of. Parents want their children to have a better life than they themselves have had and, in that, I have truly succeeded. My youngest daughter, Janet, is a senior official at the World Bank in Washington, and she has a great husband and two terrific kids. My son, David, has an MBA and a law degree and does astonishingly creative work in the financial world. As I have mentioned, Karen is a therapist who also has a great husband and two equally terrific kids.

I also have a wonderful relationship with my sister, Audrey. She now lives with her husband Steve and daughter Liz in Washington State, and we talk to one another several times a week (her other daughter, Abby, lives with her husband and daughter in Southern California, and her son, Michael, lives in Kansas). Audrey used to work as a physical therapist but is now retired and is creating amazing ceramic objects in her studio. I have several of these in my home, and I smile every time I look at them. She is a wonderful person. And it is good to know someone who really understands what I am talking about regarding my early years. She lived through that time too.

I feel that I need to say a few words about Marilyn. As I have indicated at several points in this memoir, Marilyn was a very talented, creative, and joyous person for most of her life. That all began to change when I took the professorial job at Berkeley and we moved from San Francisco to an old broken-down house in Orinda, fifteen minutes from the campus. This turned out to be a fateful, difficult move for Marilyn. Up to that time, she had always had good friends in the neighborhoods in which she lived and she thrived in teaching parent-child education classes. She even had an official state-issued certificate as an instructor in these classes, and she involved her friends in these activities. She and her friends visited each other on a daily basis. She was a happy woman. For a girl raised in a lower middle class family in San Gabriel, California, the wealthy suburb of Orinda turned out to be very intimidating for her. I once again call upon Wikipedia for a description of the town:

"Orinda is a city in Contra Costa County, California, United States. The population was 17,599 at the 2000 census. The town is located just east of the city of Oakland and home to many affluent professionals who commute to downtown Oakland, San Francisco, and Walnut Creek. The city is well known in the area as one of the most desirable addresses in the East Bay due to its excellent public schools, high-priced real estate and naturally scenic landscape. While the city is in close proximity to nearby urban areas, it has maintained a very intimate, small town atmosphere. Much of the city is very hilly and dotted with multi-million dollar custom homes. [In 2008] the median income for a household in the city was $187,637, and the median income for a family was $192,531. [The Orinda School District] is the highest ranked in California in its category according to the state Academic Performance Index."

To be blunt, Marilyn found herself overwhelmed by this fancy, expensive town, and she experienced great difficulty in finding a way to be comfortable and sociable in this setting. The town was no problem for me, of course, because I was hardly ever there. Then why move to Orinda? We knew we wanted to live in the general area of Orinda because of the great schools but we could have accomplished that goal in other less fancy nearby areas. In fact, I actually discovered a nice house in a nearby town called Moraga that I thought would be great. I got Marilyn to come look at it, and she rejected it within minutes. Why? The house was on a long, straight street with perhaps fifty identical houses lined up in a neat row, all facing the street in exactly the same way. Marilyn couldn't face this stereotypical suburban scene. She liked the house in Orinda because it was one of a kind and was nestled high in the hills with a feeling that it was all by itself. This uniqueness appealed to her. What I don't think we realized was that moving there meant that she would now be alone on the top of a hill with no neighbors. She was now isolated.

While I had worked hard earlier in my life, I basically doubled my workload in order to pay the mortgage for this house and to do the improvements that were needed to accommodate our family. For example, David had a little bedroom on the main floor of the house but we had to hire Levitch and Sons Construction Company to excavate the lower level floor so that we could provide two bedrooms down there, one for Karen and one for Janet. We also built a bathroom, laundry room, and family room on that lower level. This was an unbelievably expensive project. The house itself cost $44,500! And the improvements were another $10,000. So I worked and Marilyn, on her own, tried as best she could to "fit in." She did not do this very well. She was in a fancy neighborhood, with virtually no friends, an absent husband, a very limited budget, and challenging young children. Those were tough days.

Years later, in spite of those difficult beginnings, we could both be proud that we successfully raised three children and that we had traveled the world and made a good life together. She had supported me in getting two advanced university degrees, and she had brilliantly managed our home and family, basically on her own. On the other hand, I had supported her search for meaning in her life after she let go of singing. This search took many paths ranging from a focus on our children, to exploring her spiritual life, to building a small cosmetics operation into a thriving, home-based national import business with several employees. But in spite of all these good things, by the late

1990s, it was clear that our lives were drifting apart and that we were heading in very different directions in our lives.

In the end, after forty-four years of marriage and after several years of trying to find common ground, we could not find a way forward together and we separated in 1998. I moved out of our home in Orinda and found an apartment in a nearby community, Walnut Creek. Unfortunately, Marilyn's hopes for a new start were thwarted by debilitating health issues, and she moved in with Karen and her family who were then living in a nearby city. The Orinda house sat empty for over a year until a time came when Karen and her husband, Steve, bought it from Marilyn and me. Marilyn was now back in Orinda, the grandchildren started to attend Orinda schools, and things settled down. Several years later, Marilyn moved to Virginia at the invitation of Janet and her family. After several years in Virginia, however, her health deteriorated yet further and she died on December 1, 2006. The last chapter of our marriage did not go the way either of us envisioned it, but I know that both of us tried our best with our challenges, strengths, and weaknesses.

After Marilyn and I separated, I basically continued my life as before. I went to work and continued my teaching and research. I learned to shop for groceries and cook. I'm not very good at these things, but that's OK. I would receive a grade of "B", perhaps? I was already a whiz at doing the laundry. But I needed furniture for my apartment, and I had never dealt with that issue before. Karen took me shopping for furniture, and I think I shocked everyone when, in one single afternoon, I found many needed furniture items (sofa, dining room table, chest of drawers) at Scandinavian Designs, paid for them, and had them all shipped to my apartment. I learned later that other people can spend many weeks doing that kind of shopping, but I was happy to get it all done and out of the way.

Not everything went well or easily. I recall going to my local bank and asking to open a checking account. As the bank people were processing forms for me, I mentioned that I had a little problem and I wondered if I might have a word with the branch manager. When he appeared, I told him that I had never dealt with a bank before and I did not know the rules. What was involved in having a bank account? How does one write a check? The manager was very kind and introduced me to this new and foreign world. I am now a master. I balance my bank account every month, and if I were to be graded, I clearly deserve an "A" in this task.

Two years ago, I bought my own condominium in the hills of El Cerrito, California. The house overlooks Wildcat Canyon, and I watch cows grazing in the hills every day. Karen, Steve, and my two grandchildren helped me move in, situate the furniture, and hang pictures. Faviola comes once a month to clean the place. The house is a fifteen-minute drive to the campus, and I still go to the office every day.

25

WRAPPING UP

The phenomenon of "home field advantage" is well known in the world of sports. In team sports, a team playing in its own stadium or arena is known as the home team. The other team is known as the visiting team, and they can be said to be "on the road." Teams typically play their home games in or near their home region; they will generally have half their total games at home in a season. The home team has a significant advantage over the away team in every sport whether it is football, baseball, hockey, or soccer. And this advantage applies whether the teams involve amateur or professional players. Considerable research has been done to figure out why this is true. While many factors have been mentioned in this research, and while some controversy exists about some of the factors that have been identified, everyone agrees on the most important factor. It helps players enormously to do their best when most of the fans in the stadium are friends and supporters who applaud every move the hometown player makes.

As I have thought about my life, I have come to appreciate the power of the home team. I grew up being labeled as useless.

As we know, that can be a devastating and debilitating anchor to put around the shoulders of anyone, but especially, a young person. (And, I might add, it is even worse when the child's shoulders are narrow.) If a child internalizes the label of uselessness, it can destroy self-confidence, enthusiasm for life, and hope for a future. I was saved from that fate because of my fans in the stadium. I was mostly able to compartmentalize my father's opinion so that it did not overwhelm me. It was his opinion.

I think my fans were supportive of me because I was a good boy—I did my chores and I followed orders. Some might regard that behavior as too high a price to pay for fan support. I did not feel that way because of the alternative facing me: if my fans deserted me, I would need to accept the "useless" label. The role of a parent is to be a fan regardless of behavior. My father was incapable of that generosity, and my mother was not strong enough to engage in a battle with him. So my extended family provided an invaluable life raft. Without recognizing it at the time, I think I even chose the woman I would marry because she was a fan. But my father's behavior nevertheless colored everything I ever did later in my life. His judgments about me did not destroy me, but they certainly influenced virtually everything I have done. Even today.

I took very seriously my grandmother's advice to escape the North End because I had physical proof every day that I was doomed otherwise. If I avoided being beaten up by the Ukrainian thugs in my neighborhood, it was only because I devoted so much energy and creativity to that task. It seemed clear to me that escape from this battlefield was necessary if I were to survive. My grandmother's advice was to hang a shingle. Get an education that will allow you to do your own thing without being dependent on others. Be on your own. Do it your way. Don't follow the crowd. I took her advice to the extreme. I studied Latin declensions as if my life depended on it. I refused to do the Ph.D. thesis that was expected of me. I couldn't stay in jobs where I was not free to be free. I now see that I have organized my life so that I could hang a shingle. I live my life as I wish. I have escaped the North End of Winnipeg.

My history of emotional abuse resulted in my being extraordinarily sensitive to what others are thinking. This is a tactic abused people can use to avoid danger. This kind of interpersonal intelligence was an invaluable asset to have since I was moving from a nonintellectual home located in a working class neighborhood (where there were no accessible role models) to another life for which I had not been prepared. I had to learn a new way of thinking and of being. And I had no guideposts and road maps to help. I had to be on guard and be observant. Escaping from the North End required of me that I have self-confidence (thanks to my fan club), a motivation to escape daily beatings, and the ability, by watching and learning, to navigate an unfamiliar but demanding world.

But I think all of that is not enough. I'm not sure I would have been able to move on had it not been for my library. The library allowed me to soar in ways that would not have been possible otherwise. I could read anything I wanted. And I did. And I was able to learn about a world I never knew even existed. My parents certainly had few dreams, and they definitely did not talk to me about the possibilities available in life. My teachers in school were doing all they could just to keep order in the classroom. I'm not sure they were convinced themselves about the wonderful opportunities available if one worked hard. Like the others in my neighborhood, most of my teachers had succumbed to the neighborhood pressures. Unlike me, they had given up hope. In spite of neighborhood pressures, the library was a beacon of opportunity for me. It was full of dreams and tomorrows and promises. It said to me, "Go for it!" Add to that the stimulation and challenge of an "Oxford" education, and the pieces begin to fall in place.

John Neal (1793-1876), the poet, said, "A certain amount of opposition is a great help to a man. Kites rise against and not with the wind." Neal wrote that many years ago; current research is now showing that those who have experienced adversity in their lives subsequently have better mental and physical health than those who have not had that experience. (The exception, of course, is that overwhelming adversity is uniformly damaging.) In this account, I have tried to describe my strategies for overcoming what seemed to me to be a number of serious obstacles. But having said that, I need to emphasize that this is not a simple story with a simple message. You can damage a child quite easily in a short amount of time. To repair that damage is far more complicated, and it takes a much longer period of time. (The moral: let's do childhood better to begin with! This is my research agenda right now.)

I did manage to escape from my childhood challenges and I did manage to lead a life that I think has made a difference. The difference I have made, my greatest contribution, has perhaps been as a mentor, even though I was not consciously aware that I was doing that. I tried to help my students achieve their potential, but it was only later in my life that I was able to look back and see what I had been able to do. My inability to be aware of what I was doing is, I believe, yet another legacy of abuse. The messages I internalized were: don't think too much; don't dream out loud; keep your thoughts to yourself; help others but be quiet about it; the less said, the better. In short, stay out of sight and be safe. These were valuable messages for me, but I would not recommend them for others.

Hanging a shingle has been an important goal in my life because it has allowed me a life of freedom and independence.

But the danger of hanging a shingle is that it announces to the world that you exist. That can lead to trouble. I have hung a shingle, but I made sure it was covered with leaves and flowers so that it was not out in public view. If it wasn't for my daughter's nagging and urging, I would still be comfortably hidden from sight. But perhaps she is right. Perhaps it would be helpful for others to know that, even with only a few favorable life circumstances, you can follow your dreams and that you can improve the lives of others. Uncovering the shingle at this time in my life feels like it is a risk worth taking.

". . . I've lived a life that's full.
I've traveled each and every highway;
And more, much more than this,
I did it my way . . ."

My Way. Lyrics by Paul Anka.
Sung by Frank Sinatra.

ACKNOWLEDGMENTS

This memoir was written only because my daughter, Karen Englund, thought it needed to be written and because she never let a week go by without reminding me of the important work I had promised her I would do on it. But she did more than nag and remind and encourage. She read draft after draft and came up with brilliant insights that made sense of many of my rambling stories. She helped me understand events in my life that were totally beyond my grasp. She helped me see connections that transformed my limited imagination. I remain in awe of her brilliance.

Others contributed importantly as well. My sister, Audrey Josias, lived in the same family as I did in Winnipeg, and her comments on the accuracy of my memory during those years were invaluable. She also came up with lost and misplaced family photographs and offered details of family history and relationships. My son, David Syme, read everything and offered several penetrating insights that I found enlightening; he was also a whiz at editing my photos using his phenomenal computer skills. His help was invaluable. My daughter, Janet Piller, read the entire manuscript and offered important and useful observations, one of which led me to add additional pages to my account. Her thoughts helped broaden my perspective in many important ways. I am very grateful to Steve Englund for his creativity in designing the cover of the book.

When she wasn't looking after her brand-new baby, Dr. Laura Gottleib volunteered to read the entire manuscript and was able help me smooth out transitions, remove unnecessary words, and clarify ideas that I had managed to muddle. Dr. Sim Warkov, a veteran of the Winnipeg wars, made very helpful suggestions regarding the authenticity of my recollections. Dr. Doug Jutte was chauffeur on my recent trip to Winnipeg and took pictures of me in the Carnegie Library. Dr. Megan Galbally, a psychiatrist friend from Melbourne, Australia, offered several penetrating and thoughtful comments about the early life of children. Claudia Schwarz also read the entire manuscript and offered very helpful suggestions that helped me clarify the role of parents in raising their children.

I benefited from all this support and help in more ways that I can say. It's good to have a home team advantage.

As anyone can tell from reading my story, I think of libraries as a major resource for stimulating the imagination of children. To me, this is especially true for children living in underprivileged communities. A portion of any money that may be realized from the sale of this book will therefore be donated to library organizations in such communities.

Printed in Great Britain
by Amazon